IN SEARCH OF THE BEYOND

By the same author

Letters from the Desert
The God Who Comes

IN SEARCH OF
THE BEYOND

CARLO CARRETTO

translated by

SARAH FAWCETT

DARTON, LONGMAN AND TODD

First published in Great Britain by
Darton, Longman and Todd Ltd
89 Lillie Road, London SW6 1UD

This translation © Darton, Longman and Todd 1975

Originally published as
Al di la delle Cose
by Cittadella Editrice
Assisi, Italy
Reprinted 1977 (twice), 1979, 1981 and 1983

All biblical quotations are from
THE JERUSALEM BIBLE
© 1966 Darton, Longman and Todd Ltd and
Doubleday and Company Inc.

Set in Intertype Baskerville

Printed and bound in Great Britain by
Anchor Brendon Ltd, Tiptree, Essex

ISBN 0 232 51291 4

CONTENTS

6 *Contents*

PART III 113

PROLOGUE

People have asked me whether, in times of protest like our own, I too might find something to protest about.

I have nothing against protest, indeed, I am all in favour of a bit of activity; I like to see a young man jump up on to a table and spontaneously deliver an impassioned tirade against something he feels is wrong and should be put to rights.

What is there to reproach him for?

Surely we are all agreed that things are not as they should be.

A member of the older generation, wedded to the established order and to principles of economy, may be anxious lest window-panes and furniture should begin to fly back and forth with the words – and I have in fact been told that in one far-eastern country the students virtually razed their old university building to the ground, so intense was their anger and the violence of their protest. But now that I am approaching death, and since I am familiar with the language of the Apocalypse, the cost of one building makes little impression on me compared with the cost of the great devastation at the end of time.

Besides, life has taught me one thing : that he who protests loves, and he who protests much loves much. There is only one thing I have never managed to understand : why those who are challenged do not come out into the open as well, into the very centre of the fray, and cry out with all their strength : 'You are right, brothers, things are going badly, and it is our fault. You are right to rebuke us. We have made bad use of our power, we have abused your trust. Forgive us and help us to change.'

Above all, I cannot understand why there are thinking people who get upset, ecclesiastics who are shocked, and so on, when people protest against the Church, and make use of hallowed phrases like 'living the Gospel', 'we must be poor', 'we must return to the sources'.

I would go down to the market place clad in sackcloth and ashes and say quite simply : 'You are right, my sons, we have forgotten Jesus, and deviated from his teaching. We need to change and become converted; we must effectively build up a Church which will be the Church of the poor, the charismatic Church, the Church of the Spirit, the Church . . . '

How splendid such a universal protest would be, a world-wide protest in which fathers and sons would take hold of one another crying, 'We are all blackguards !' A protest in which priests and people would unite in a single cry, a common prayer : 'Our fathers sinned, and we have sinned ourselves, we are all sinners'. In the end we would have sinned ourselves, agreement on one point which is basic to man's life on earth, and which it is good to recall from time to time : we are not perfect; the Church is the Church of sinners; each one of us is moving onwards towards perfection, but . . .

Here we might ask ourselves a question.

What is the underlying reason for the fact that our generation sets out so persistently and energetically to emphasize that things are going badly? The answer is that preceding generations, with equal persistence and energy, took every opportunity to say how well everything was going, especially in the Church.

I remember when I was a schoolboy and reading history books for the first time. It was not difficult to see that certain crimes had been committed by persons of consequence – this cleric, for example, or that pope.

Overcome with doubts, home I would go to express my bewilderment. The invariable response was a cuff from my mother, who, with her conditioned respect for clerical language and dress, would tell me, 'You don't criticize the parish priest.'

If I went to the parish priest and told him that in all conscience I could not understand how Pius IX had failed to grasp certain details in time . . . and so on, the heavens would open. I would find myself listening to a sermon on the Church, holy and spotless, without wrinkle or blemish, and I would return to school with that narrow, prejudiced outlook which has been such a cause of scandal to intelligent, open-minded individuals in our own day.

What we need now is patience, a great deal of patience, and we must endure – though without fear – the choppy seas that will inevitably rock the Church.

If we do so, besides realizing that we are all sinners, that it is important that we should keep ourselves in humility, we shall come to understand something else : that the Church is not in men's hands, but in the hands of God, and that he alone – not we men who in our presumption think we are safe and secure simply because we are in the Church – has power to still the wind and calm the waves.

But it is not with men that I want to take issue.

I am filled with compassion for them.

All of them.

Nor is it with myself. I have already gone in for too much self-scrutiny; so much so, in fact, that I became discouraged about the possibility of ever achieving anything worth while.

I pity myself, too, and I assure you that I am sustained now by the theological virtue of hope, not by confidence in any virtue of my own; it is faith in Jesus that lights up my night, not faith in myself or my own faculties, which are weakening with the onrush of time.

I want to take issue instead with God, with my God.

With the One who has pursued me ever since my childhood and still pursues me.

The One whom I learned to know and love in the Church of my adolescence and youth, so rich in mystery and feeling, in colours, ornaments and lights.

The One who drew me into the desert in order to purify my faith and strip my altars bare, who led me under the Cloud of Dark Knowledge of himself that I might sense his Mystery, his Darkness, his Silence and his Transcendence.

The One in whom I have recognized the God of Abraham, the God of the prophets, the God of the Psalms, and above all the God of Jesus Christ and his Gospel, the God who is living in the Church and in the Eucharist, yesterday, today and for ever.

The God who is the source of my being, who is with me and around me, and who draws me into the unfathomable abyss of his own designs, towards the vision of himself, which will be eternally new.

He is the one with whom I want to take issue.

What is more, I am not the first to do so, and I know there is one particular kind of protest that is pleasing to him.

I mean the protest that springs from love. He is always ready to listen to that.

Did he not listen to the protest of Abraham, his friend? When, outside Sodom, God revealed to the patriarch his intention of destroying the city, Abraham made this protest:

' "Are you really going to destroy the just man with the sinner? Perhaps there are fifty just men in the town. Will you really overwhelm them, will you not spare the place for fifty just men in it? Do not think of doing such a thing: to kill the just man with the sinner, treating just and sinner alike! Do not think of it . . ." Yahweh replied, "If at Sodom I find fifty just men in the town, I will spare the whole place because of them."

'Abraham replied, "I am bold indeed to speak like this to

my Lord, I who am dust and ashes. But perhaps the fifty just men lack five : will you destroy the whole city for five?" "No" he replied, "I will not destroy it if I find forty-five just men there." Again Abraham said to him, "Perhaps there will only be forty there." "I will not do it" he replied "for the sake of the forty."

'Abraham said, "I trust my Lord will not be angry, but give me leave to speak : perhaps there will only be thirty there." "I will not do it," he replied . . . ' (Gen 18 : 23–30).

And so on as the figure gradually decreases in a dramatic exchange in which one thing is at stake : the salvation of those men. It is precisely about this that I want to protest. No longer capable of finding any alternative approach, I want to take issue with God in defence of contemporary man. I want to act like that other formidable protestor, Moses, who, when confronted with God's plan to destroy his idolatrous people in the confines of the desert, said to him : ' "Yahweh, why should your wrath blaze out against this people of yours whom you brought out of the land of Egypt with arm outstretched and mighty hand? . . . Leave your burning wrath; relent and do not bring this disaster on your people. Remember Abraham, Isaac and Jacob, your servants, to whom by your own self you swore and made this promise : I will make your offspring as many as the stars of heaven . . ." So Yahweh relented and did not bring on his people the disaster he had threatened' (Ex 32 : 11–14).

This the the kind of challenge that pleases God, and I too would have recourse to it, rather than sit back insisting that things are going badly and that the world deserves to be destroyed.

In the end, of course, by saving others I save myself, which is obviously not a matter of indifference to me.

My reasoning is simple :

Mankind today is in the desert, just as the people of God were with Moses on the mountain. Now, as then, men are demanding meat instead of manna. And now, as then, men have fashioned for themselves a golden calf.

So what is one supposed to do?

Start talking about destruction and punishment, like some uninspiring hack preacher?

Or beg God to teach man a lesson?

There is no need for that.

We are quite capable of punishing ourselves, and as far as destruction is concerned, we already have at our disposal all the means necessary for wiping mankind off the face of the earth.

And, in any case, the rainbow still spans the heavens at high noon after the rain, a reminder that the destructive flood was an experience of humanity's childhood, while now . . .

Yes, now humanity no longer looks on itself as a child, it has achieved adulthood. And adults cannot be threatened with disasters. Even when they do occur, people no longer look on them as coming from God. Theirs is a world from which God is absent. They may not have reached a point of total denial but they cannot conceive of God as having any interest in human concerns, as being involved in the details of daily life. The Bible, which is the one book which really marries heaven and earth, still lies on their tables, but they misguidedly persist in searching through it for an alternative reading – an adult reading.

They have begun to react against the dense veil of unsophisticated imagery that surrounds the things of God and women and sin and the world beyond, and they endeavour to tear it aside with a display of self-assurance that is frankly infuriating.

Poor things! They do not realize that by tearing aside that veil of symbolic language, which in its very simplicity conveys all the mystery of God and of things, they will find themselves naked and unprotected in the actual presence of the Mystery. They will no longer understand anything at all.

Nor will they see anything.

The Mystery is a light more blinding than thousands of simultaneously exploded atomic bombs.

If you attempt to gaze on it directly, you are blinded and enter into a darkness that is your own, not God's. He knew this, and devised for our sake certain precautionary measures. Christ knew it, and issued his terse warning: 'Unless you change and become like little children you will never enter the kingdom of heaven' (Mt 18 : 3).

This is the crux of the matter, and knowing the danger to which my generation is exposing itself, I wish to take issue with God.

I am not afraid that God will destroy the world, but I am afraid that he may abandon it to wander blindly in the sophisticated wasteland of contemporary civilization.

I am not afraid that he will allow us to want for food and medicines, but I am afraid that he may abandon us to the temptation against faith. I will not presume to say that I have experienced the terrors of the night of the spirit, and I do not know whether that night is the same as the one described by St John of the Cross. I only know that it is a terrible experience to find oneself with one's faith exposed before the stark Reality of God.

And there is one way, and one only, of coming through the experience : the way of childhood, littleness, humility, persevering prayer, tears. It is not easy, I admit, because before resolving to become little we are only too inclined to try every other way imaginable. In nearly every case the way of humility and tears is chosen only when one feels defeated and at a loss where to turn. The parable of the wedding feast described by Luke tells how, in order to have his table full, the king finally commanded his servants, 'Go to the open roads and the hedge-rows and force people to come in . . .' Lk 14 : 23). And it is sad to think that we possibly begin to search for God only because we no longer know where else to go, and only when, let down by beauty, by health and by our dreams, we are prepared to open ourselves to the One who still loves us, and makes use of our misfortunes to compel us to enter at last into the kingdom of his love.

This is why I want to challenge my God.

Lord, my God, pity your people, and do not be over-severe with them. I realize that as a result of the riches of the land in which they live, and the pleasure it gives them, your people no longer hunger after the promised land; but, Lord, be patient for a little while more; you will find they will come to understand in the end.

I know that they spend too much time trying to reach the stars that you yourself call by name, and leave so many of their brothers to die of hunger, but, Lord, you will see that some good will come of it. You will see that from the port-hole of some space ship one of them will celebrate your greatness. To see a man standing on the moon and hailing the earth that you have loved so intensely, and for which you gave up your life – surely that is something beautiful, Lord?

Lord, have pity on man.

I have confidence in him, even though he has revealed himself to me in all his colours.

One thing I ask you, above all. Do not try his faith beyond the limit, do not put him through that overwhelming test.

If he *will* get himself into all kinds of trouble through his childish, arrogant desire to know everything, by all means chastise him, but do not abandon him to his darkness.

I fear for the man who no longer knows where his God is.

Make him aware of your touch through his experience of created things, make him recognize your presence behind the veil of all present realities.

Lord, bring upon us all the misfortunes that, in your justice, you might have prepared for us, all except that of being the last witnesses to the Invisible.

PART I

'And he did this so that all nations might seek the deity and, by feeling their way towards him, succeed in finding him. Yet in fact he is not far from any of us' (Acts 17 :27).

Chapter One

RETURN TO THE DESERT

The goodness and merciful love of God have led me back to the desert. During the day my eyes feed on the light from the stupendous sand-dunes of Beni Abbès; and at night I spend hour after hour absorbing the peace that pours down from the stars, strewn in myriad profusion throughout the galaxy. Its lambent glow seems to have been created expressly for me as a strong sweet reminder of the luminous Cloud of the Dark Knowledge of God while I make my journey through the desert of life. I feel happy, as never before, happy to the point of tears.

And as they fill my eyes the world becomes more compelling in its beauty than ever, and in the depths of my being I am aware of the movement of God.

In such moments everything seems to remain suspended in an eternal present, while the many miles that separate me from my 'yesterday' contrive to deepen the 'mist of forgetfulness' of things, releasing in me the joy of finding myself alone with Him, the Eternal, the Infinite, the Transcendent, and strengthening my resolve to break for a while with everyday things in order to give myself in complete self-surrender to the Absolute.

The desert, in biblical thought, is not a goal but a passing stage, which is how Elijah understood it: 'he walked for forty days and forty nights until he reached Horeb, the mountain of God' (I K 19 : 8). The exodus from slavery to freedom takes place in the desert: 'Remember how Yahweh your God led you for forty years in the wilderness, to humble you, to test you and know your inmost heart – whether you would keep his commandments or not. He humbled you, he made you feel hunger, he fed you with manna which neither you nor your fathers had known, to make you understand that man does not live on bread alone but that man lives on everything that comes from the mouth of Yahweh. The clothes on your back did not wear out and your feet were not swollen, all those forty years.

'Learn from this that Yahweh your God was training you as a man trains his child, and keep the commandments of Yahweh your God, and so follow his ways and reverence him' (Dt 8 : 2–6).

In the Gospel the desert marks a period of preparation for Christ as he stands on the threshold of his active mission : 'Immediately afterwards the Spirit drove him out into the wilderness and he remained there for forty days and was tempted by Satan. He was with the wild beasts, and the angels looked after him' (Mk 1 : 12–13).

It provides some respite from the pressure of the crowd : 'Then he said to them, "You must come away to some lonely place all by yourselves and rest for a while" ' (Mk 6 : 31).

It is a milieu suited to prayer : 'After sending the crowds away he went up into the hills by himself to pray' (Mt 14 : 23); or to prolonged meditation : 'Now it was about this time that he went out into the hills to pray; and he spent the whole night in prayer to God' (Lk 6 : 12); or to quench the thirst for absolute aloneness with the Father : ' "Stay here while I pray." And going on a little further he threw himself on the ground and prayed that, if it were possible, this hour might pass him by. "Abba [Father]" ' (Mk 14 : 32–35).

If the prophets did so, and if Jesus did so, we too must go out into the desert from time to time.

It is not a question of transporting oneself there physically. For many of us that could be a luxury. Rather, it implies creating a desert space in one's own life. And to create a desert means to seek solitude, to withdraw from men and things, one of the undisputed principles of mental health.

To create a desert means learning to be self-sufficient, learning to remain undisturbed with one's own thoughts, one's own prayer, one's own destiny.

It means shutting oneself up in one's room, remaining alone in an empty church, setting up a small oratory for oneself in an attic or at the end of a passage in which to localize one's personal contact with God, to draw breath, to recover one's inner peace. It means occasionally devoting a whole day to prayer, it means going off into the loneliness of the mountains, or getting up alone in the night to pray.

When all is said and done, creating a desert means nothing more than obeying God. Because there is a commandment – arguably the most forgotten of all, especially by the 'committed', by militants, by priests – and even bishops – which requires us to interrupt our work, to put aside our daily tasks and seek the refreshing stillness of contemplation.

'Remember the sabbath day and keep it holy. For six days you shall labour and do all your work, but the seventh day is a sabbath for Yahweh your God. You shall do no work that day, neither you nor your son nor your daughter nor your servants, men or women, nor your animals nor the stranger who lives with you. For in six days Yahweh made the heavens and the earth and the sea and all that these hold, but on the seventh day he rested' (Ex 20 : 8–11).

Do not be afraid that your momentary withdrawal will be detrimental to the community; and do not be afraid that an increase in your personal love for God will in any way diminish your love for your neighbour. On the contrary, it will enrich it.

Let us here recall something which is both important and awesomely true : loving our fellow men, devoting ourselves to the human community with which we must totally identify, achieving a humble, vital understanding of the poor – these are demanding, exhausting undertakings. Only a strong personal love for God can effectively sustain and preserve them in all their freshness and divine newness. It is man's nature to harmonize these two loves, to fuse them into a balanced dialectic. Even the closest and most demanding relationships – mother and son, or husband and wife – require periods of absence, moments of separation, precisely in order that those involved should come to a new and deeper appreciation of the forces that bind them together.

'Place the tents far apart, draw near with your heart', says the Tuareg proverb, and if this applies to the nomad, accustomed to wandering freely through uncharted territory, imagine how much more true it must be for us westerners, living like sardines in our high-rise flats, and hemmed in by the crowd.

It is man's destiny to be alone; that is why he needs to train himself, prepare himself, become mature enough to 'stand alone'. And the desert was designed expressly for this maturing process. To refuse to accept the desert is to deny the vertical dimension of existence – one's relationship with God, the need for prolonged prayer, the face-to-face exchange with the Transcendent.

I would be unhappy if the great emphasis laid on the community aspect of Christianity, the shift away from yesterday's individualism, the joy of praying together in a renewed liturgy, were to flourish to the detriment of the solitary aspect of our existence. Among many young people and progressive priests today we find a very realistic awareness of the fact that God reveals himself to us in the very act of love by which we establish, live in and develop our communities, but I would not wish this to signify the abandonment of the arduous path of personal prayer, which alone can bring us to a fully mature union with God and mature contemplation. I would hope, finally, that in heeding Christ's words, 'for where two or three meet in my name, I shall be there with them' (Mt 18:20), we shall not allow ourselves to forget those other words of his, 'When you pray, go to your private room' (Mt 6 : 6).

Those who make Christianity a purely personal affair are certainly mistaken, but those who are willing to consider only the horizontal implications of Christ's teaching would be equally mistaken. This would turn the Gospel into a socio-logical tract, and it would lose its savour. The truth stands at the precise point where the two dimensions meet. It is not for nothing that the symbol of Christianity is the cross – the realization of the two loves, even on the material level, lived out until martyrdom : love of the Father and love of one's brethren.

Chapter Two

THE PARABLE OF CREATION

This morning I have come out on to the dunes before sunrise. Yesterday's wind has carefully combed and smoothed the sand, and the traces of its passage over the ridges are there in all their splendour and mysterious freshness. The ocean of sand stretches out before me as far as the horizon, where the dawn light heralds the coming of day.

There are few sights in nature so unspoiled as a sea of dunes under the blue sky of the Sahara ! It is like seeing the beginning of creation and the spiritual content is so powerful that the visible and the invisible are perceived as a single reality.

Sand and sky separated by a single horizontal line : nothing else.

Yet it is the parable of creation which begins to unfold here, revealing its underlying meaning.

No simple, innocent, childlike eye, opening on to this sight, could possibly be in danger of doubting.

God is here, just as you are here, and the sand and sky are here.

You can start speaking to him immediately.

This is the way in which he is present.

The very elements that go to make up the scene are his words. His speech is contained within things, his thought is expressed in the reality that surrounds me.

Everything is a symbol which introduces me to the dark knowledge of him and prepares me for something that is to come, and yet is already come.

I feel him there, searching me out, coming to meet me, I feel him embracing me already, like someone who has been waiting for a long time, knowing that I would be coming.

Filled with grateful love, I reach out to touch that beauty which in his beauty, I ponder the harmony which is his harmony, I stand spellbound by the newness which is his newness. And it is easy for me to say to him :

> 'Bless Yahweh, my soul.
> Yahweh, my God, how great you are !
> Clothed in majesty and glory,
> wrapped in a robe of light !
>
> You stretch the heavens out like a tent,
> you build your palace on the waters above ;
> using the clouds as your chariot,
> you advance on the wings of the wind ;
> you use the winds as messengers
> and fiery flames as servants'
>
> (Ps 104 : 1–4).

God presents himself to you like this. Welcome him.

A horizontal line with a bit of sky above and a bit of sand below is all that is needed.

And yourself before it, watching, watching, watching.

Do not ask for anything, just contemplate. Do not let yourself be led astray by the evil tendencies of your heart.

Can you not see that your heart is sick from its own cunning and would rather interrogate than contemplate. Already, instead of remaining in ecstasy, it wants to rebel. Totally wrapped up in its own doubts, it does not even give your eye time to scan the full sweep of the horizon before demanding a sign from the Invisible one who is present, saying, 'Give me a different sign from the one you have given me.' Why do you do this, my heart? Are the signs that already surround you not enough?

Can he show any greater power than the power he has shown in creating? Can he increase the perfection of the perfection he has already given, or the beauty of the beauty that is already there? Why does my heart react like this?

No, I will not ask him for another sign. The things I can see are enough. No one asks his own mother for a visiting card as he emerges from the womb; that would be tactless to say the least. My mother is not required to introduce herself to me in order to explain who she was before I appeared on the scene.

And by the same token I ask no sign from my God who is present in his creation, immanent in things and yet transcending them.

Indeed, I will rely on the signs he leaves of himself, signs that will not fail to guide me in my search, but bearing in mind one very important thing, a kind of *sine qua non* for all relations with the Transcendent One : 'Unless you change and become like little children, you will never enter the kingdom of heaven' (Mt 18 : 3).

This saying of Christ is straightforward enough, but it also contains a warning : you will never enter, never enter, never enter.

But then what?

If this doorway into the Invisible is closed to me, where will I find one that is open?

If I cannot enter the kingdom, where will I find refuge?

But now be peaceful, my soul, stop thinking about the warning that made you tremble.

Contemplate what lies before you.

It is God's way of making himself present.

A horizontal line with a bit of sky above and a bit of sand below is all that is needed.

The sand is the symbol of visible realities, the sky of those that are invisible. I say symbol, because in fact the sky is not any more invisible than the earth.

It is the same thing.

The invisible is neither on earth nor in heaven.

The invisible is the transcendent, the *beyond*, the other side of creation's fabric.

The invisible is the possibility to create visible things freely.

The invisible is all that did not need to be created, the Eternal, the Unchangeable.

The invisible is God.

And why is he invisible?

It is not because he enjoys hiding from you, but because you are as yet unable to see him. You will see him later.

Do you want a comparison?

Go backwards, backwards in time, and imagine yourself in your mother's womb.

Enclosed within the womb, you can touch your mother with your feet, with your hands, with your whole body. You are aware of her, you feel and touch her, but you do not see her.

The time for that has not yet come.

But can you really have any doubts about her – her presence, her reality? Even though you cannot see her.

You began life in your mother's womb, and in all beginnings there are things – many things – that must be accepted without understanding.

Only faith and hope can throw any light on the beginning : faith, which is the eye of the reality you cannot see, and hope, which is the conviction that you will be born when it is time.

In the beginning you have a thousand ways of experiencing the presence of the one who will bring you to birth, but you must accept your limitations, your own immaturity, inexorably bound up with the passage of time which does not belong to you and whose child you are.

Your moment will come!

And when it does, after the lightning flash of the Apocalypse, you will emerge from the womb of time, along with the rest of creation.

Then you will see God face to face, you will touch the Tran-

scendent with the finger of your love. No comparison has helped me as much as this one to understand the reason for the
darkness of faith, and why we must remain small before the
mystery of Being.

We live in the womb of things, in the womb of history and
the contingent; we are immersed in the process of becoming.

Only the Apocalypse, at the end of time, will open up to us
the vision of the divine Transcendence, of the *beyond*, and
then we shall see God face to face.

But then everything will be complete and explained.

In the meantime there is nothing to do but wait.

In fact, living is waiting.

Now I turn back to look at the tenuous line of the horizon, lit
up now by the sun which, in the meantime, has risen before
me.

The sand becomes pale ochre in colour, and the sky, dominated now by the masterful presence of the sun, loses something
of its transparency.

I no longer seem to see creation as it was at the beginning,
but creation as it will be at the end.

This sand which runs through my fingers is all that remains
of past history, of the civilization which flourished in a Sahara
that was once alive, teeming with life.

Some of these civilizations have left a record of themselves,
superb, incredibly well-preserved inscriptions, evidence of a
high degree of development.

Now cities and villages alike have disintegrated. The sun
and wind of the Sahara have reduced them to sand, mountains
of sand.

Nothing has been able to resist the relentless rhythm of time,
the searing wind which consumes the granite.

Will the steel of our own technological civilization be able
to resist any better?

Will the vast complex world we know today be able to resist? The civilized world of science and culture?

And the others that are still to come, the civilizations of the future, will they hold out against the forces of time, against the sun and the wind?

No, they will not resist. New York, Paris, Moscow, Peking, Athens, Rome, all will become like these sand dunes.

It may be that the heat will simply be replaced by cold, the cold of the end of the world.

Everything will be reduced to sand, because sand is the symbol of death, and everything must die.

Some people imagine the possibility of a connection, or better, some kind of real continuity, between the level of technology and maturity reached by human civilizations and the kingdom of God. But they are wrong, there is no such continuity.

The kingdom belongs to a different order.

If there *is* any connection it is a symbolic and not a real one. If there is a link it is in the fire of love, and in the white heat of the charity we drew on for the difficult task of constructing the earthly city.

The new heavens and the new earth which have been promised by the Spirit and form the substance of our faith will be truly new, and not just the old things remade as if new. God is not waiting for anything from us before he re-fashions, re-creates, heaven and earth. His new work in no way depends on the stage we may have reached.

What do you want him to wait for?

Seeing that he himself said, in a moment of sadness : 'But when the Son of Man comes, will he find any faith on earth?' (Lk 18 : 8).

Do you expect him to wait when we are possibly on the verge of blowing the world up with one of our atomic bombs?

God is God, and he is God precisely because he has no need of anything we may have to offer (Ps 117 : 27). Our technology will end up in the sand, just like the first wheel constructed by some gazelle hunter on these same Saharan plains.

Our sociology will end up in the sand, just as the legislation of the ancient civilizations finished in the sand. I am making a new heaven and a new earth, says Christ in the Book of Revelation, and it is as if he were saying : I am making another universe because the old things have passed away. And faith consists in believing that God has this power.

At this point I can well imagine that some people are worried, even scandalized. I hear them say : 'What is the good of all our efforts, our exertions, our work? Will anything remain of the earthly city?'

Yes, love will remain.

The house will disappear, but the affection that held us together will remain. The workshop will disappear, but the toil and sweat which earned us our bread will remain. Human revolutions will be forgotten, but tears shed in the cause of justice will remain. Our old bodies will disappear; the wounds of our sacrifice and the scars of our struggles will remain – but in newly created bodies, transparent and divine; we will be sons of the resurrection and no longer the slaves of death. Indeed, a first pledge of this hope is given us in the resurrection of Christ.

This is why the fact of the resurrection of Jesus assumes such significance in the Good News as preached by his first companions. If Christ is risen, the question of my own joy, fulfilment and happiness no longer presents any problem. It is all a question of waiting.

Waiting, in fact, is what my history, my prayer and my hope are all about. Now I kneel down, and opening the Book of Revelation I read :

'Then I saw a new heaven and a new earth; the first heaven and the first earth had disappeared now, and there was no longer any sea. I saw the holy city, and the new Jerusalem, coming down from God out of heaven, as beautiful as a bride all dressed for her husband. Then I heard a loud voice call from the throne, "You see this city? Here God lives among men. He will make his home among them; they shall be his people, and he will be their God; his name is God-with-them. He will wipe away all tears from their eyes; there will be no more death, and no more mourning or sadness. The world of the past has gone."

'Then One sitting on the throne spoke : "Now I am making the whole of creation new," he said. "Write this : that what I am saying is sure and will come true." And then he said : "It is already done. I am the Alpha and the Omega, the Beginning and the End. I will give water from the well of life free to anybody who is thirsty; it is the rightful inheritance of the one who proves victorious; and I will be his God and he a son to me" ' (Rv 21 : 1–7).

'The Spirit and the Bride say, "Come." Let everyone who listens answer, "Come." Then let all who are thirsty come : all who want it may have the water of life, and have it free.

'The one who guarantees these revelations repeats his promise : I shall indeed be with you soon. Amen; come, Lord Jesus' (Rv 22 : 17–20).

Chapter Three

THE POOR OF YAHWEH

What creation tells me is only a beginning.

The revelation conveyed to me by heaven and earth in their splendour, their immensity and their harmony, marks no more than the beginning of a dialogue which will go on for a long time, occupying me throughout my life here, and beyond.

I should add immediately that while this dialogue has a beginning, it has no end, because the two speakers, God and man, are eternal and are to live in the same dwelling.

It would be strange to live in the same house without speaking to one another, and stranger still not to know one another.

Yet man has been created to know God, to speak with God.

The knowledge may be slow or quick to develop, the dialogue with him may prove easy or difficult to sustain, but I would say that ultimately neither can be avoided.

It is almost impossible to dissociate oneself from the plan of God, which is precisely this, 'that all nations might seek the deity and, by feeling their way towards him, succeed in finding him. Yet in fact he is not far from any of us, since it is in him that we live, and move, and exist' (Acts 17 : 27).

No, God is not far from any one of us, he is with us and he always has been.

If we have learned to recognize his presence in creation, then we will find it embodied in his Revelation; if his word has reached us through the symbolic language of what we see, it will penetrate our spirit through the mystery of the Word.

Scripture will bring fulness to the message of the mountains, the seas and the stars; the Bible will draw man into this dialogue with God.

The Book of Genesis and the Wisdom literature will bring out the meaning of the dawns and sunsets. The story of Abraham and the Book of Job will throw light on the mystery of suffering.

The Book of Exodus will draw attention to the slavery of sin, and through the proclamation of the Law the waywardness of man's heart will be corrected.

In the miracle of the Red Sea man will discover the possibility and the hope of salvation, and in the Song of Songs the why and the wherefore of love.

He will find in the Psalter the language of prayer, and in the mysticism of the prophets the vocation to intimacy with the Eternal.

Yes, the mystery of creation finds in the Bible a book that is worthy of it, while the Bible finds in Nature the most conclusive witness to its truth.

In the hands of God, both contribute as one to the dialogue with man; together they serve him as receivers, on which he picks up the wavelength of his God in the eternal spaces of Being.

What, then, is God saying to man through creation?

What is God saying to man through the Scriptures?

One thing and one only : that God is God and man is man.

The consequences follow of their own accord; what matters is that man should realize that God is God and that man is not God.

It may seem almost absurd to keep on insisting on this truth, but it is not so : for our mistakes, our uncertainties and our unhappiness almost always stem from our having ignored one or other term of the equation.

To acknowledge that God is God is to achieve complete peace, to enjoy an optimistic outlook on life; it means believing that everything is regulated by the loving omnipotence of a Being who will lead everything to its goal, and who, being God, is the eternally New, and in whose presence every creature will quench its thirst and achieve its own fulfilment.

Ultimately it implies *adoration* which is simply the jubilant response to creation, the smile of the son towards the father, the joyous and trusting approach of one who has not towards the One who has, of one who cannot towards the One who can, of thirst towards the source, of nothing towards the All. I would suggest that the deepest and the most comprehensive truth which emerges from the contemplation of nature as *the belief that God has created and is creating* and of the Scriptures as *faith that God has revealed and is revealing himself* is this : that man is the poor one of God, that man is rightly defined as *the poor one of Yahweh.*

This expression 'poor', which nature teaches you to understand in terms of hunger, need, sweat, drought, sickness and death, which the Bible will enrich with its thought, its prayer and its experience, and which Jesus will make his own with exile, hard work and the harsh realities of daily life, is without any doubt the most complete, comprehensive and authentic one of all, placing man in the presence of his God, the creature in the presence of his Creator.

> 'Listen to me, Yahweh, and answer me,
> poor and needy as I am ;
> keep my soul : I am your devoted one,
> save your servant who relies on you'

(Ps 86 : 1–3).

The poor of Yahweh !

How rich in meaning these words are for the man who lives in God, who seeks God and loves him.

It is a peace-bearing phrase, a ray of light, a piercing shaft of love. This unassuming, humble attitude of supplication and dependence wraps the soul round like a cloak, shines like a lamp to light up the way, and serves as a staff for the journey through the desert.

It causes his prayer to well up within him :

> 'I waited and waited for Yahweh,
> now at last he has stooped to me
> and heard my cry for help.
> He has pulled me out of the horrible pit,
> out of the slough of the marsh'
>
> (Ps 40 : 1–2).

> 'I love you, Yahweh, my strength . . .
> Yawweh is my rock and my bastion,
> my deliverer is my God.
> I take shelter in him, my rock,
> my shield, my horn of salvation'
>
> (Ps 18 : 1–2).

It becomes the driving force behind all his rejoicing and praise of God :

> 'God, you are my God, I am seeking you,
> my soul is thirsting for you,
> my flesh is longing for you,
> a land parched, weary and waterless,
>
> (Ps 63 : 1).

The unshakable basis of his peace :

> 'In God alone there is rest for my soul,
> from him comes my safety;
> with him alone for my rock, my safety,
> my fortress, I can never fall'
>
> (Ps 62 : 1–2).

> 'Yahweh, our Lord,
> how great your name throughout the earth !

B

Above the heavens is your majesty chanted . . .
I look up at your heavens, made by your fingers,
at the moon and stars you set in place –
ah, what is man that you should spare a thought for him?'

(Ps 8 : 1, 3–4).

The inexhaustible source of his prayer of petition :

'Look after me, God, I take shelter in you.

To Yahweh you say, "My Lord,
you are my fortune, nothing else but you" '

(Ps 16 : 1–2).

His constant yearning :

'As a doe longs
for running streams,
so longs my soul
for you, my God'

(Ps 42 : 1).

The most reliable place of refuge in times of danger :

'Save me, God ! The water
is already up to my neck !

I am sinking in the deepest swamp,
there is no foothold'

(Ps 69 : 1–2).

The realization that God is his goal :

'God, you are my God, I am seeking you.'

Man is the poor one of Yahweh, and Jesus, who is the perfect
man, will stand before God, in the name of all men, as *the
poor one of Yahweh. Blessed are the poor*, and he will trans-

form what was originally an attitude of painful submission into one of joyful, loving acceptance. It is rightly said that humility is truth, in which case, the truth that God is God creates humility in man's heart, and this humility serves as the foundation of the entire spiritual edifice.

Man before God is the poor one *par excellence*.

But he is a poor man who can rely on Another to satisfy his needs.

This is the source of that attitude, characteristic of the poor man who has the courage to go on asking even for what seems impossible.

David asks that he might conquer Goliath with the power of five stones and a sling.

Joshua, that he might bring down the walls of Jericho with the crooks of shepherds who have come from the desert.

There is no limit set on the request. Everything depends quite simply on the maturity that has been achieved through faith, and on absolute confidence in the power of God.

The poor man is really poor, but the poor of Yahweh has God at his disposal.

The realization of this is enough to make one's head spin.

God at the disposal of my faith ! What an awesome thought !

Jesus has left us an echo of that sense of vertigo. We are told in the Gospel of his being tempted by the possibility of changing stones into bread, or of casting himself from the pinnacle of the temple without doing himself any harm.

He says himself that he recovered his equilibrium by crying out in the midst of temptation : 'You must not put the Lord your God to the test' (Mt 4 : 7).

Yes, it is a terrible thing to feel that God is at the disposal of our poverty.

All things are possible for him who believes. That is the secret of the poor of Yahweh.

I am nothing, but God is my all.

I have nothing, but God is the fulness of being and I will lose myself in him. I believe this is the most radical experience man can have here on earth, the most dramatic struggle man can have with God, the face-to-face encounter of Israel with Yahweh in the night of the Passover under the moon of bare faith. And I also believe that nothing gives greater glory to God than this struggle on the bastions of the invisible; and that nothing gives him greater consolation than this cry which springs from the mouth of man who is caught up in the struggle with no weapon other than his own weakness, but with unshakable confidence in God's will to involve himself in what concerns him as a poor man.

I feel such a strong sense of brotherhood with all those people who have been and are aware of their radical neediness, but who yet believe in *the God of the impossible.*

Brother of Abraham, poor in his old age, impotent and alone, but trusting in the promise that is to make him the father of many nations.

Brother of Moses, who, inwardly aware of his vocation to liberate his people, had nothing but the poverty of a motley crowd of shepherds with which to confront the army of Pharaoh.

Brother of Job, who, having become, on his miserable dunghill, the very incarnation of poverty, would give evidence before the whole world of his proven faith. 'This I know : that my Avenger lives' (Job 19 : 25).

I am bound, in fact, as a brother, to all the poor, the destitute, the starving, the weak, the sinful, the despised, who have no one to rely on but God. But, above all, I am the brother of Mary, who had the courage to offer to God the poverty of her humble nature as an insignificant and unknown woman when confronted with the dark mystery of becoming the mother of Christ, and the constancy to accompany him unquestioningly to the Cross, to the ill-treatment, spittle and blood.

Chapter Four

THE POOR MAN PUT TO THE TEST

There is not only the vertigo that comes from feeling the power of God within our grasp; unfortunately we experience the same sense of vertigo when, as everything becomes dark ahead of us and his light is obscured behind the storm clouds of trial, we cry out that we no longer believe in him. Nothing is more self-evident than the existence of God and nothing is more obscure; nothing causes us greater elation than the feel of our hand in his, and no darkness is more painful than our moments of bare faith. Through faith we believe that God created the world, and theorizing about it can help us, but it is not enough. We can truly say that all the proof needed to demonstrate his presence to us is there already, and at the same time be terrified at the thought that nothing further can be added to shake our incredulity.

Faith is neither a feeling nor a mental process; it is an act of self-surrender in the dark to a God who is indeed darkness as far as our human nature is concerned. And he is darkness not because of an absence of light, but rather because we are overwhelmed by the reverberations of a light to which we are as yet unaccustomed, here in the restricted world of our own unfolding history.

The area in which reason and faith operate, and in which there is an interplay of light and shadow belonging to the two clearly distinct worlds, the visible and the invisible, is a terribly complex one. When the light which emanates from the Cloud of Unknowing reaches the earth on which we are journeying,

it forms, as it were, a *mist* (St Paul) which surrounds everything and forces us to *feel our way* (Acts), putting us on our
guard and inducing within us a continual state of anxious
expectation.

An expectation which obliges us to fix our gaze on what
lies ahead, and gives us a glimpse of the unexpected patch of
sunlight which is to come. And it is on this uneven terrain
that, sooner or later, God will be waiting for us, as he waited
for Abraham, as he waited for Moses, as he waited for Job.
Normally God leaves us to live in our tents, like the young
Isaac under the eye of his father. As cherished sons in our
Father's house, he leaves us to enjoy our laughter and to run,
glad and carefree, on the hills of a life that is rich in peace
and every other blessing. In moments like this we have no
doubts about him and faith comes as easily as the heartbeat
of the young, as the deep healthy breathing of those who are in
good health. But one day . . .

' "Take your son," God said [to Abraham], "your only child
Isaac, whom you love, and go to the land of Moriah. There
you shall offer him as a burnt offering, on a mountain I shall
point out to you" ' (Gen 22 : 1–2).

This is the moment of testing.

The skies darken, and faith is as starkly naked as the un-
covered blade which cuts the flesh.

And then one says to oneself : 'Is it possible that a God of
love could demand such a sacrifice? Perhaps faith is just a
trap? A psychological illusion? Is it possible when children
are dying of hunger, when the innocent are being killed and
the wicked man triumphs? When earthquakes destroy the
houses of the poor and drought reduces further still what little
rice they have? This is the moment of testing, the moment of
scandal ! And in the face of our anguish heaven remains closed
and hostile and our question unanswered.

Why, Lord?

Why, Father?

Why, my God?

But this God whom we are invoking has taken up a challenge – a challenge in which we ourselves, without wishing it or perhaps even realizing it, are the stakes.

'Satan said [to God]: "But Job is not God-fearing for nothing, is he? Have you not put a wall round him and his house and all his domain? You have blessed all he undertakes, and his flocks throng the countryside. But stretch out your hand and lay a finger on his possessions: I warrant you, he will curse you to your face" ' (Job 1 : 9–11).

It was Satan who initiated the challenge, and God is caught, as it were, in a trap.

'Perhaps it is true that Job only believes in me and loves me because I have showered him with blessings and filled his life with joy?'

And so it is that God abandons Job to adversity and he is harshly afflicted with every kind of material adversity. The challenge is accepted; Job loses his flocks, his sons are killed, his lands laid waste.

But what is Job's own response to all these misfortunes?

' "Naked I came from my mother's womb, naked I shall return. Yahweh gave, Yahweh has taken back. Blessed be the name of Yahweh" ' (Job 1 : 21).

But the challenge is taken still further, and Satan says to God : ' "Skin for skin! A man will give away all he has to save his life. But stretch out your hand and lay a finger on his bone and flesh. I warrant you, he will curse you to your face" ' (Job 2 : 4–5).

The trial of strength intensifies, and God still accepts the challenge in man's name : ' "Very well, he is in your power. But spare his life." So Satan left the presence of Yahweh.

'He struck Job down with malignant ulcers from the sole of his foot to the top of his head. Job took a piece of pot to scrape himself, and went and sat in the ashpit. Then his wife said to him, "Do you now still mean to persist in your blame-lessness? Curse God, and die." "That is how foolish women talk," Job replied. "If we take happiness from God's hand, must we not take sorrow too?" And in all this misfortune Job uttered no sinful word' (Job 2 : 7–10).

Job did not sin, he affirmed his faith, and by repeating his conviction : *I know that my Avenger lives,* in the midst of such dreadful trials, was to bear witness before all men – a witness as enduring and resplendent as any precious stone.

Naked and covered with sores, like the man who survives the night of the senses and passes through the night of the spirit, Job succeeded in reaching the frontiers of the invisible, there to gaze through his tears at the horizon were the sun is on the verge of rising.

But how hard it is !

St John of the Cross speaks of the great compassion we should feel for *those who remain in the night,* those who suc-cumb to the powerful attraction of the senses, or are led astray by spiritual pride and cast themselves to the ground howling and cursing; for those, sick with rationalism, who bring the canons of reason into matters of faith and claim they can break into the stronghold of the mystery with the pocket knife of reason; that they can look into the light of *the dark knowledge of God* with their short-sighted human eyes.

For this precisely is our tragedy : we think we know, when in fact we know nothing; we think we can see, when in fact we are blind. What do *we* know of death, of eternity, of the purpose of things, of suffering, of what was before us, of what will be after us?

We imagine we have a plan, when in fact we have not; we believe we know what is good for us, when all the time we may be working to destroy it.

All too often, our one concern is to remain at home undis-turbed, however dull and joyless it may have become.

We are afraid of adventure, of the new and the mysterious.

If it were left in our hands, we would ask God to stay here on our level, when all the while our happiness depends on our moving upwards towards him.

We would willingly ask him to spare us all suffering, though it is genuinely for our good that we should suffer a little.

We know nothing, or practically nothing, about our eternal destiny, and we cling so tenaciously to what we believe is for our good. Affluent and overfed ourselves, we think that the only evil in the world is hunger; because *we* get upset by pain and privation, we think that the only problem to be resolved is that of providing bread and better hygienic conditions for the Third World. Of course these are serious problems for which solutions must be found, but what we fail to recognize is the far greater wretchedness of some rich people who die of boredom and drugs in comfortable bourgeois houses, and who stifle their personalities beneath their accumulated wealth and their self-centredness.

What we lack is true perspective, and this distorts the whole picture of our lives.

When all is said and done, we still believe that our home is here on earth, and that death, which takes us away from it, is somehow a mistake.

But the reality is diametrically opposed to this, and it is useless for us to try and alter things. The earth, whether we like it or not, is *not* the ultimate reality, and one day we shall discover that death was an invaluable and wise friend.

Is it not so?

This is the truth, this is the mystery, the one immense mystery in which we are all involved, and it is useless to worry about it, to complain, to wish things were otherwise : this is how things are.

We live surrounded by the contingent, the provisional; we are caught up in the process of evolution, of becoming, and the restlessness that clings to us like a second self is the sign of this. As I said earlier, we are still in the womb which is pre-

paring us for birth, and anyone who is still in the womb is
not in a convenient position to look into the face of the one
who bears him.

It is necessary to trust, to believe, to hope, to accept.

Ultimately it is a question of patience because, as Scripture
says, 'Your endurance will win you your lives' (Lk 21 : 19).

Besides – and it is time this was said – if this earth were the
goal of creation, we really would have something to complain
to God about, and could legitimately hand him the prize for
incompetence as creator.

My knowledge may be limited, but I know enough not to
be satisfied with what I see around me or, worse yet, with
what is within me.

To be so would be absurd, a great mistake, a cause for
scandal even. How could one understand death if earth was
one's home and one was taken far from it? Who would not
blaspheme in the face of innocent suffering, the ruthlessness of
tyrants, the disasters produced by hostile nature? As if to relieve
God of his responsibility, or else driven by an unshakable and
incurable optimism, there are those who say : 'It is true that
things are going badly, but we only have to get together in a
spirit of goodwill, and the situation will improve; with the
help of our doctors we might even succeed in overcoming death;
we will certainly not have any more starving people, and with
our technology we will build a habitable world – or one that
is reasonably so'.

And then, just at the crucial moment, an earthquake swallows
up entire cities at a time, or seasonal disasters reduce to nothing both the hard work of millions of poor people and the economic calculations of governments. There is obviously something here which does not quite add up and causes me to
doubt the efficiency or goodness of God himself.

No, Job was right : 'Yahweh gave, Yahweh has taken back.
Blessed be the name of Yahweh.' And Anna was right when
she said, 'Yahweh gives death and life, brings down to Sheol

and draws up; Yahweh makes poor and rich, he humbles and also exalts' (1 S 2 :6–7). God is not the reliable protector we imagine him to be according to the negative, domestic dimensions of our faith; he is a demanding God who, in order to heal me, is quite capable of crushing me, and who, to save an entire people from paganism, can abandon them to exile, hunger and nakedness. *God gives, and God takes back* – a hard truth for someone to swallow who has accustomed himself to a sort of lightning-conductor God, a wonder-worker who cures personal ills; or to a theology of limited range, largely developed in *ex voto* shrines and merely concerned with rational explanations of the mystery, ready to justify a God who might send you to hospital or leave you unemployed.

God has absolutely no need to be justified by our theological pretensions. There is no point in attempting to justify him before the mystery of things that do not turn out as we would like them to.

And it is a waste of time to place all the blame on Adam. In any case, he is not here to listen to us. Whether we like it or not, it is all part of the mystery of God, it is God who gives and who takes away, and until we can get back into the way of attributing to him – as does Job and the Bible – both what is good and what is evil, without getting bogged down in a morass of casuistry whose sole purpose is to evade the mystery, we will never succeed in making a radical act of faith. As long as we are accustomed to see the evils from which we suffer as no more than the work of evil men, we shall only learn to hate them and try, like Marxism, to overthrow them.

Marxism is evil only in so far as it involves a direct denial of the Transcendent, and, in building up society, completely excludes all agents apart from man. And what a lot of Marxism has seeped into the lifeblood of contemporary Christianity!

Not in the sense that there are Christians who are tempted to engage in guerrilla warfare and to approve the use of violence, but in the sense that they have been penetrated by a more subtle poison.

'Do not look to God for bread, look rather to governments, technicians and silos.'

'What has God to do with the cultivation of fields, with the productivity of the earth, with chemical fertilizers?'

They have become 'enlightened', 'up-to-date', 'liberated' from the sacred, which attributes certain powers to the blessed water used on rogation days or to the prayers of some unlettered woman.

They have stepped out of the world of mystery and can no longer recite the Our Father meaningfully because they no longer believe that God intervenes or even wants to intervene in such banal human concerns as the harvesting of rice.

In fact, they have replaced the Our Father with words that make more sense, and have credited technicians with a greater power than they actually have. *You* give us this day our daily bread.

But the technicians do not always succeed in doing so, and things end up in a mess.

If there is one prophecy that should be proclaimed loud and clear in the leaden sky of contemporary rationalism it is this : 'Listen, Israel : Yahweh our God is the one Yahweh.' He is the God of the impossible, the mysterious God who has rescued you from the powers of darkness and hatred and led you to the land he promised to your fathers (Deuteronomy).

Believe in him, place your trust in him. He rescued you from the land of despair and doubt and led you into the desert in order to purify your heart. Do not be afraid, Israel, saying : what are we to eat, what are we to drink now that we have become so numerous that the land seems incapable of containing us all.

Is my arm shortened or my power diminished? Yahweh asks. Come, put me to the test – go to the temple and pray – give up your evil ways, sever your links with impiety and usury, and then come to me, and you will find out whether or not I am able to pour out on your heads a torrent of blessings, the overflowing river of my bounty (Zechariah).

Do not be afraid, Israel, I am with you. When you pass through fire and water, call on me and I will save you. When you see the dry bones strewn on the vast plains of death, trust in me. Those bones will rise. The Lord has spoken (Ezekiel).

I am your God, and there is no other.

From the rising of the sun to its setting, so wide is my mercy towards those who fear me and call on my name.

I am God, yesterday, today and forever.

We have therefore reason for weeping when the voice of prophecy is silent in the Christian community, or when prophecy itself is reduced to merely human dimensions.

It means that the poor one of Yahweh is betraying his God, placing his trust in man instead.

But what will we say when the Gospel is reduced to sociology, and pastors become mere political agitators or organizers of 'good works'?

Who will prophesy then?

Who is going to say that bread is a gift from God when even the priests regard it as a gift from the Americans, and Christians think they can have it in greater quantities simply as a result of careful planning?

Never more, perhaps, than today have we run the risk of reducing the Bible, and the Gospel in particular, to a guide for good behaviour, a belated support for democracy and the equality of all men.

If he follows this road, the poor one of Yahweh will be overwhelmed by the duplicity of men, and having strayed from the path that led him to the desert where his heart could be purified, he will die of hunger and thirst far from God.

May God forbid!

Chapter Five

THE BEYOND

Here we come to the heart of the matter, to the precise point where faith – and not only faith – plays its determining role and provides the answer for anyone who tries to penetrate the beyond. The Book of Job, and everything that we have said so far, only makes sense if, having enabled man to penetrate the heart of things – and nothing can do so more effectively than suffering and love – it brings him out of the experience quickened with renewed life. Things have been given to us that we may penetrate them, but through the dynamic process of becoming, we come out on the other side of them towards the Infinite, the Eternal, the Unchangeable. We know that nothing can stop short man's course in the world of the contingent, the temporary, and that there is a goal which surpasses everything, drawing us towards a point in which everything will be accomplished and explained.

It is like the descent of turbid, impetuous torrents towards the great ocean of peace. The restlessness of Ulysses, the Greeks' awareness that everything is in a state of flux, and most of all, the eschatological perspective of biblical thought, are all indications of this fact. There is one book in the Bible which is perhaps the most important as a witness to the unsatisfied longing of the human heart in its never-ending search for that which is : the Book of Ecclesiastes.

It is a strange book, almost too easy to read, but not so easy to understand.

When I was young, and was introduced to the Bible for the

first time, I was quite surprised that the Church had included this among the canon of inspired books. I felt it was a pagan book, slightly dangerous.

Now that I am older and somewhat more experienced in the search for unity and the synthesis of all things, I must admit that it is one of the books that I find most persuasive. For if Job bears witness to the existence of God beyond, and in spite of his suffering, Ecclesiastes bears witness even more powerfully to God's existence beyond pleasure. He had the courage to say : this life is tedious . . . can you not see? You insist that you like it? I tell you that it no longer has any interest for me. You still feel the pull of the pleasures of this world? For myself, I am fed up with them.

It is precisely in human pleasure, in the delights that the world offers me, that I have discovered the emptiness of things and the thirst for something totally different !

How it rings true, this book of wisdom ! Listen.

'I thought to myself, "Very well, I will try pleasure and see what enjoyment has to offer." And there it was : vanity again ! This laughter, I reflected, is a madness, this pleasure no use at all . . .

'I did great things : built myself palaces, planted vineyards; made myself gardens and orchards, planting every kind of fruit tree in them. I had pools made for watering the plantations, bought men slaves, women slaves; had home-born slaves as well; herds and flocks I had too, more than anyone in Jerusalem before me. I amassed silver and gold, the treasures of kings and provinces; acquired singing men and singing women and every human luxury . . .

'I then reflected on all that my hands had achieved and on all the effort I had put into its achieving. What vanity it all is, and chasing of the wind ! There is nothing to be gained under the sun' (Ecclesiastes 2 : 1–11).

It takes courage to say things like that, especially in a piece of sacred writing, and they can only be said – if they are not to become blasphemy – if the speaker is fully aware that the new reality he is looking for, the good he seeks as the one thing necessary, belongs to another dimension, is further on, existing beyond the realities of this world. The expression *there is nothing to be gained under the sun* can only be used by the man who has already made the earth his own, just as the opinion that culture is of little significance can only be held honestly by the man of culture, and only the rich man and the artist can say that riches or art are trifles.

Otherwise it is impertinence or superficiality. Life is understood by the man who is dying, and things are appreciated by someone who is giving them up or giving them away.

This is how Ecclesiastes sings of the approaching disappearance of created things :

'Light is sweet; at sight of the sun the eyes are glad. However great the number of the years a man may live, let him enjoy them all, and yet remember that dark days will be many. All that is to come is vanity.

'Rejoice in your youth, you who are young; let your heart give you joy in your young days. Follow the promptings of your heart and the desires of your eyes.

'But this you must know; for all these things God will bring you to judgment.

'Cast worry from your heart, shield your flesh from pain.

'Yet youth, the age of dark hair, is vanity. And remember your creator in the days of your youth, before evil days come and the years approach when you say, "These give me no pleasure", before sun and light and moon and stars grow dark, and the clouds return after the rain; the day when those who keep the house tremble and strong men are bowed; when the women grind no longer at the mill, because day is darkening at the windows and the street doors are shut; when the sound of the mill is faint, when the voice of the bird is silenced, and song notes are stilled, when to go uphill is an ordeal and a walk is something to dread.

'Yet the almond tree is in flower, the grasshopper is heavy with food, and the caper bush bears its fruit, while man goes to his everlasting home. And the mourners are already walking to and fro in the street before the silver cord has snapped, or the golden lamp been broken, or the pitcher shattered at the spring, or the pulley cracked at the well, or before the dust returns to the earth as it once came from it, and the breath to God who gave it.

'Vanity of vanities, Qoheleth says. All is vanity' (Ecclesiastes 11 : 7–12, 8).

No, the earth no longer interests me. I am weary of it. It gives me increasingly less pleasure. I remain just as long as I need to remain in order to learn to love, to pay something towards the cost of the redemption, but it no longer attracts me as once it did. I have come to realize that it is in my interest to move on. And this is an important sign.

I am familiar with the changing seasons of life, I have lived through its loves, I have rejoiced in each as it dawned. Now I am looking round for yet other seasons, for another love, for another dawn.

I have lived down here long enough to convince myself that we were not made for the earth, that the earth is not our paradise, and that it has been of service to us only as a great preparation for something else. Above all, it carries within it the all-too-familiar seeds of decay, and as the years pass I find it increasingly wearisome, while my soul fixes its sights with assurance on the One who always has the power to captivate, the uniquely, truly and eternally new : God.

Yes, conceived in Genesis by the love of God, we attain self-awareness in Exodus, consciously and painfully collaborating with God, and we are brought forth at last into eternal life beyond the Apocalypse, beyond history, when all things will have delivered their message and each one of us made his choice freely.

So man's basic condition here on earth is one of waiting, he is at home with insecurity, suffering characterizes his everyday experience and his hope lies in the final transformation of all things. The efforts made by each succeeding generation to create a state of earthly happiness and stability inexorably come to grief after the first few attempts, leaving in their wake a more pronounced lack of self-confidence in man and a pessimism more bitter than even death itself. What does retain its validity is the goodwill of 'men of goodwill', together with the love that went into the effort to create, and the increasingly manifest approximation to the divine model of the Kingdom in which every man is a man and all men are equal, but . . . how can this man be satisfied with things on an earthly scale, when God has planted in the depths of his being the awe-inspiring seed of the divine and opened up before him the infinitely vaster, more perfect perspectives of the Kingdom of God? If, as Christ has said, the Kingdom is already within us, how can man possibly still his longings in the realm of his own humanity, however beautiful, however fascinating it may be?

Sooner or later he will break through the barrier and gallop through the fields like a thoroughbred that has been enclosed for too long within the narrow confines of its stable.

Once he becomes aware of his true nature as a son of God, how can he be content to be no more than a son of man?

This is the real source of man's restlessness, of his unconscious urge to search for novelty, of his desire to discover the beyond and breach the walls of the invisible.

We have germs of eternal life within us, seeds of divine life. Such germs or seeds, though planted within our human nature, must now begin to germinate, put down roots and bear flowers and fruit in an unfamiliar soil that does not belong to this earth at all, and which is defined in the Gospel as 'the Kingdom'.

Already there is blood flowing within me that I have inherited neither from my mother nor from my father, but directly from God.

In short, the supreme truth, the most exhilarating piece of news, the most disconcerting fact is this : *I am not simply the poor one of Yahweh, I am the son of Yahweh.*

This sonship is not juridical, it is real. Born a child of man, I am reborn in grace, a child of God.

This is not just playing with words; it is a fact, the basis of our greatness and our motive for hope.

Do you believe in evolution?

I do myself, and I became an evolutionist, not by studying the skeletal structure of prehistoric animals in order to observe the successive stages in the great chain of being, but because I experienced it within myself. I became aware, in the depth of my being as a man, of the tension, the *evolution* of becoming a son of God. Through my own religious experience I came to realize that the phrase 'son of God' is neither rhetorical, nor symbolic; it describes a reality.

At this point perhaps I may be permitted a short digression by way of illustration. I recall that Mgr Olgiati told me a similar story when he wanted to explain to me what it means to be an adopted son of God. It was his stock story, and I shall now tell you mine. At Tazrouk in the Hoggar the Little Brothers had a fraternity among the ex-slaves of the Tuareg, poor families who lived by cultivating a bit of grain and a few vegetables along the *oued*.

The *oued* of Tazrouk was a haven of peace and the brothers too had their garden, where they worked the soil.

But what a labour it was to draw something forth from that sand! If there was not a drought, the locusts descended, and if one escaped the locusts there were caterpillars instead. And what is more, rabbits used to come in from round about and make short work of the little bit of green that had been acquired as the result of so much effort.

By way of self-defence, therefore, one was compelled to set traps, and these became the source of a bit of meat which was generally not too bad – as long as it was not fox or jackal.

One evening a flight of storks appeared in the sky above Tazrouk, bound for the north : it was spring at the time.

Descending in wide circles, the birds came to pass the night on the *oued*. In her efforts to find somewhere to alight, a beautiful female stork put her foot right into one of the traps. All that night she lost blood, and when the dawn came, and her companions realized what was happening, it was too late. All attempts to save the poor bird were useless : she died that same day and we buried her at the edge of the *oued*.

But then began the drama which involved each one of us intimately. The flight of storks set out once more for the north, but the partner of the dead stork stayed behind at the *oued*. That evening we saw the wretched bird come down near the garden, in the same place that his partner had been trapped, and fly round and round, crying and showing by obvious signs that he was looking for something. This went on until sunset. The same scene was repeated next day. The flight of storks had possibly reached the Mediterranean by now, and yet this lone bird was still there, searching for his companion. He stayed for the entire year. Each day he would go off in search of food, and at sunset we would see his outline against the sky over the garden, as he came down in the usual place, crying, searching and finally going to sleep in the sand where, perhaps, he could still detect the smell of his partner's blood.

The brothers became accustomed to the stork, as he did to them. He would fly into the garden and come over to take whatever morsel of meat or moistened bread the brothers offered him.

It was moving to see how sensitive this creature was to the love and attention of the brothers, who, feeling themselves to be somehow responsible for his bereavement, redoubled their attentions.

I remember the look in his eyes, his habit of cocking his head on one side, the regular movement of his beak, and the way he had of staring at me, as if he were trying to catch hold of me and escape from his solitude.

I for my part tried to understand him, but I remained myself, and he remained a stork. I remained imprisoned within my limitations as he did within his – limitations fixed for us by nature.

There was no possibility of communication.

And yet this migrant had done, and knew how to do, extraordinary things, things that I myself would have been incapable of doing.

He had left the hot countries – Mali, perhaps, or Niger – and he had travelled hundreds of miles with neither compass nor radar; he was capable of continuing his journey without a map, until finally he came back to the same roof-top, the same chimney-pot as last year and there built his nest. And yet . . . for all his skill as a long-distance navigator, he would not have known how to read my language or interpret the intonation of my voice.

The following spring another flight of storks reached the *oued* of Tazrouk. This time our friend joined it, and set out once more for the north.

I have often thought about that bird as I searched for a comparison or tried to explain the gulf that exists between the nature of animals and the nature of man. Comparisons are of limited value, but they can help us in our weakness.

There is also an unbridgeable gulf between the nature of God and the nature of man – there is the fact of transcendence.

And herein lies the mystery kept hidden, as St Paul says, through many centuries, and revealed to us in the fulness of time.

God, in his love, decided to bridge the gulf, making it possible for man to become in every respect his son.

It is as if, with a power I do not in fact possess, I had some-

how enabled the stork to achieve the impossible and become
my child, and therefore capable of 'understanding me', of 'com-
municating with me', of living my life, sharing my intelligence,
my love, my will.

For to confer a nature, to establish a parent–child relationship, does not simply require a legal act recorded in a ledger
in a registry office; in reality it means ensuring that the one
who is adopted as 'son' can share the same preferences and
customs as his father; that he can share his parent's nature
– which means sharing the power of perceiving, loving and
willing. This is the mystery : what theologians call our
participation in the divine nature, and which St Paul cele-
brates in the Epistle to the Ephesians when he recapitulates
the plan of God.

'Blessed be God the Father or our Lord Jesus Christ, who
who has blessed us with all the spiritual blessings of heaven in
Christ. Before the world was made, he chose us, chose us in
Christ, to be holy and spotless, and to live through love in his
presence, determining that we should become his adopted sons,
through Jesus Christ for his own kind purposes, to make us
praise the glory of his grace, his free gift to us in the Beloved'
(Ep 1 : 3–6).

John also describes it in the magnificent prologue to his
Gospel :

'But to all who did accept him, he gave power to become
children of God, to all who believe in the name of him who was
born not out of human stock or urge of the flesh or will of
man but of God himself' (Jn 1 : 12–13).

Born of God, I who was born of a man and a woman whom I
learned, from my earliest years, to call mother and father!
What a profound mystery! Nicodemus was right to be per-
plexed by Jesus's statements.

How can one bridge the unbridgeable?

Given the fact that God offers us such a priceless gift, how are we to make it a reality for ourselves? How can we turn it into something authentic, living, true?

If God was prompted by love to make so radical an offering, how could man respond adequately? How could he freely make it his own?

Who would show us the Father's house, familiarize us with his language, his customs, his will?

Who, in short, would 'reveal' God to us?

Enable us to approach the heart of his inexpressible knowledge?

Make it possible for us to make the transition to another nature which spelled complete darkness in terms of our understanding, our language?

Who would overcome the problem of God's otherness, bridge the gulf that separates creature from Creator, man from God?

Who would make it clear to me what I ought to do?

Who would pass on to me his own life, his personal knowledge?

Listen...

Chapter Six

JESUS

'O unsearchable mystery! God has taken our human nature, he has deigned to be born of the Virgin in order to make us sharers in his own divinity' (Liturgy of Christmas).

In order to achieve the impossible, the God of the impossible took the first step himself. What man was unable to do for himself on his journey towards God, God has done by stooping down towards man. To enable man to take his place in the family of God, God entered the family of man. With the Incarnation for the first time the unbridgeable was bridged from above to below. Something that had never happened before – that One from above should come down to us – happened in Jesus.

The invisible became visible, the intangible became tangible in Christ. History has been shocked into new life since Jesus came to play a part in it: the cosmos has become a sacred offering since the Word took flesh from a woman living within the cosmos.

God has become man, the Word has become a child, Immensity has accepted limitations.

The infinite has become finite.

The unknowable has made himself known.

Omnipotence became a child.

The immutable accepted suffering.

The Perfect one took on the burden of sin.

Life was attained through death.

Love was expressed as resurrection.

Jesus became our brother.

What happened is so amazing that it leaves us speechless with wonder; the fact is unique enough to justify our incredulity. And we should not be surprised if many people remain puzzled. We should be surprised by the contrary.

In order to proclaim that God became man, we need the invincible courage of faith.

In order to believe that Jesus is the Christ, the Son of the Living God, we need a revelation from the Father.

We need absolute humility of mind and heart if we are to enter into such a mystery as this. There is no point in discussing it.

Leave men to seek and to love, and they will find.

Each of us has his own history; each must follow his own path with patience and perseverance. Sooner or later our history, our path will meet up with, and intersect the history of Jesus, the path along which he is travelling.

Then – but only then – comes the moment of choice, of acceptance, of the yes or the no. One thing, however, is certain : until we have accepted him and borne our witness that he is the Son of God, something will be missing from our life, for us the sunlight will be mixed with shadows, at dawn we will be filled with nostalgia, and our nights will be restless.

It is inevitable !

If you have ever met anyone who has found the answer to the mystery of life or peace of heart, without Jesus, come and tell me about him, for I have never come across such a one.

As for me, I began to know Jesus as soon as I accepted Jesus as the truth; I found true peace when I actively sought his friendship; and above all I experienced joy, true joy, that stands above the vicissitudes of life, as soon as I tasted and experienced for myself the gift he came to bestow on us : eternal life.

But Jesus is not only the Image of the Father, the Revealer of the dark knowledge of God. That would be of little avail to me in my weakness and my sinfulness : he is also my *Saviour*.

On my journey towards him, I was completely worn out, unable to take another step forward. By my errors, my sinful rebellions, my desperate efforts to find joy far from his joy, I had reduced myself to a mass of virulent sores which repelled both heaven and earth.

What sin was there that I had not committed? Or what sin had I as yet not committed simply because the opportunity had not come my way?

Yet it was he, and he alone, who got down off his horse, like the good Samaritan on the way to Jericho; he alone had the courage to approach me in order to staunch with bandages the few drops of blood that still remained in my veins, blood that would certainly have flowed away, had he not intervened.

Jesus became a *sacrament* for me, the cause of my salvation, he brought my time in hell to an end, and put a stop to my inner disintegration. He washed me patiently in the waters of baptism, he filled me with the exhilarating joy of the Holy Spirit in confirmation, he nourished me with the bread of his word. Above all, he forgave me, he forgot everything, he did not even wish me to remember my past myself.

When, through my tears, I began to tell him something of the years during which I betrayed him, he lovingly placed his hand over my mouth in order to silence me. His one concern was that I should muster courage enough to pick myself up again, to try and carry on walking in spite of my weakness, and to believe in his love in spite of my fears. But there was one thing he did, the value of which cannot be measured, something truly unbelievable, something only God could do.

While I continued to have doubts about my own salvation, to tell him that my sins could not be forgiven, and that justice, too, had its rights, he appeared on the Cross before me one Friday towards midday.

I was at its foot, and found myself bathed with the blood

which flowed from the gaping holes made in his flesh by the nails. He remained there for three hours until he expired.

I realized that he had died in order that I might stop turning to him with questions about justice, and believe instead, deep within myself, that the scales had come down overflowing on the side of love, and that even though all men, through unbelief or madness, had offended him, he had conquered for ever, and drawn all things everlastingly to himself.

Then later, so that I should never forget that Friday and abandon the Cross, as one forgets a postcard on the table or a picture in the worn-out book that had been feeding one's devotion, he led me on to discover that in order to be with me continually, not simply as an affectionate remembrance but as a living presence, he had devised the Eucharist.

What a discovery that was!

Under the sacramental sign of bread, Jesus was there each morning to renew the sacrifice of the Cross and make of it the living sacrifice of his bride, the Church, a pure offering to the Divine Majesty.

And still that was not all.

He led me on to understand that the sign of bread testified to his hidden presence, not only during the Great Sacrifice, but at all times, since the Eucharist was not an isolated moment in my day, but a line which stretched over twenty-four hours: he is God-with-us, the realization of what had been foretold by the *cloud* that went before the people of God during their journey trough the desert, and the *darkness* which filled the tabernacle in the temple at Jerusalem.

I must emphasize that this vital realization that the sign of bread concealed and pointed out for me the uninterrupted presence of Jesus beside me was a unique grace in my life. From that moment he led me along the path to intimacy, and friendship with himself.

I understood that he longed to be present like this beside each one of us.

Jesus was not only bread, he was also a friend.

A home without bread is not a home, but a home without friendship is nothing.

That is why Jesus became a friend, concealed under the sign of bread. I learned to stay with him for hours on end, listening to the mysterious voices that welled up from the abysses of Being and to receive the rays of that light whose source was in the uncreated light of God.

I have experienced such sweetness in the eucharistic presence of Christ.

I have learned to appreciate why the saints remained in contemplation before this bread to beseech, to adore and to love.

How I wish that everyone might take the Eucharist home, and having made a little oratory in some quiet corner, might find joy in sitting quietly before it, in order to make his dialogue with God easier and more immediate, in intimate union with Christ.

But still that was not enough.

Jesus did not overcome the insuperable obstacle presented by the divinity and enter the human sphere simply to be man's saviour. Had that been all, his work would have remained unfinished, his mission of love unfulfilled.

He broke through the wall surrounding the invisible, and came down into the visible world to bear witness to 'the things that are above', to reveal to us 'the secrets of his Father's house', to give us in concrete form what he called eternal life.

What exactly is it, this famous 'eternal life'?

He himself defined it in the Gospel : 'And eternal life is this : to know you, the only true God, and Jesus Christ whom you have sent' (Jn 17 : 3). So eternal life is, first and foremost, knowledge. It is a matter of knowing the Father, knowing Jesus. But it is not a question of any external, historical, analogical knowledge which we could more or less imagine, possess perhaps, even now; it is rather a question of real, supernatural knowledge which, although it is still surrounded here by the darkness of faith, is already the same as the knowledge we will have when the veil is torn aside and we see God face to face. It is a question of knowing God *as he is*, not as he may appear to us or as we may imagine him. This is the heart of the mystery I have tried to describe as *the beyond*, and which is the key to the secret of intimacy with God and the substance of contemplative prayer.

In giving us 'eternal life' Jesus gives us that knowledge of the Father which is already our first experience of living, here on earth, the divine life; which is a vital participation, here and now, in the family life of God; and which means that while we remain sons of man, we are at the same time sons of God.

Then there is the knowledge of Jesus. We will never find words adequate to describe what the simple phrase 'to know Jesus' contains and means for us.

For God established Christ as a bridge between heaven and earth, between the seen and the unseen; he constituted Christ as author of salvation and teacher of his brethren; as the restorer of the original plan of the Father and the one before whom every knee should bend, on earth, in heaven and under the earth.

Jesus is the Image of the Father, the centre of the universe and of history.

Jesus is our salvation, the radiance of the God we cannot see, the unquenchable fire of love, the one for whom the angels sigh, the Holy one of God, the true adorer, the eternal High Priest, the Lord of the Ages, the glory of God.

Jesus is also our brother, and as such he takes his place beside us, to teach us the path we must follow to reach the invisible. And to make sure that we understand, he translates into visible terms the invisible things he has seen – as man he acts as

God would act; he introduces the ways of the family of God on to the earth and into the family of man.

All this is called the 'Good News'.

Whatever Christ does as man in the Gospels, it is as if God were doing it in heaven.

What Jesus says in the Gospels is what he has heard the Father say in heaven.

The Gospel is the way in which we can live here on earth as the saints would live in heaven.

The Gospel is everything.

It is the unique model; it is invisible perfection made visible in Christ's manner of life.

For a Christian there should be no other book from which to draw inspiration, no other model to imitate.

The Gospel is a living person : Jesus Christ.

If the Gospel prefers poverty to riches it means that the Father sees things this way, and will judge us according to his standards, not ours :

If the Gospel looks for mercy and forgiveness it means that such behaviour is habitual with God and we should bring our own actions into line with it.

If the Gospel believes in the Resurrection there can be no reason for doubting it.

If the Gospel shows preference for the simple life of the poor, of shepherds and artisans, so much so that it wanted the Son of God to be poor, a humble workman, those of us who are not poor, simple workmen must look to ourselves. We could be in for some nasty surprises.

If the Gospel tells us that it is better to find oneself minus an eye or an arm in the kingdom of heaven, than physically intact in hell, we should get used to paying less attention to our appearance and concentrating more on our salvation.

If the Gospel tells us we are sons of the Father in heaven what reason have we for doubting it?

Why not be at peace and rejoice?

PART II

'Be happy at all times; pray constantly; and for all things give thanks to God' (I Th 5 : 17).

Chapter Seven

THE RUSSIAN PILGRIM

I have discovered a really extraordinary story, and I want to tell it here.

It is about a young Russian, born in a village in the Ural province. Having been orphaned at the age of three, and lost an arm when he was seven, he had one unique blessing – his grandfather who taught him to read the Bible.

A series of misfortunes punctuated his youth: his house was destroyed by fire, and tuberculosis deprived him of his young wife.

He kept to his hovel, weeping.

Then he felt he could no longer go on living where he had suffered so much and where his memories were so painful.

He gave what possessions he had left to the poor, took a knapsack in which he put a bit of dry bread and a Bible, and became a pilgrim. For thirteen years he walked the roads of Russia, living on alms and visiting monasteries and churches; he accustomed himself to living in the solitude of the steppes and fields, and he had one great desire: to be able, one day, to reach Jerusalem.

We meet him, when he is thirty-three, the Lord's own age. Let us allow him to speak for himself – it is more interesting:

By the grace of God, I am a man and a Christian. In my life a great sinner; my status, homeless pilgrim; general circumstances, poor and perpetually on the move from place to place.

As for possessions, I have a knapsack on my back with dry bread in it, and a Bible in my pocket. That is all.

On the twenty-fourth Sunday after Pentecost I went into a church to pray during the Office. Someone was reading from St Paul's First Epistle to the Thessalonians, where he says 'pray constantly'.

These words made a great impression on me, and I wondered how it was possible to pray constantly, given the fact that everyone was bound to be involved in a certain number of activities in order to support his life. I looked it up in the Bible, and there I read with my own eyes exactly what I had heard during the Office. It is necessary to pray constantly (I Th 5 : 17), to pray in the Spirit on every possible occasion (Ep 6 : 18), in every place to raise one's hands up reverently in prayer (I Tm 2 : 8).

However much I reflected, I did not know what decision to make. How, I said to myself, can I set about finding someone to explain these words to me? I will make the rounds of the churches where there are well-known preachers, and perhaps I will find what I am looking for.

And I set out on my journey.

From then on I heard many excellent sermons on prayer, but they were instructions about prayer in general – what prayer is, why it is necessary to pray, what are the fruits of prayer. But how to pray constantly – nothing was said about that. I even heard a sermon on the prayer of the heart and on continual prayer, but no one suggested to me how such prayer could be achieved. So attendance at sermons failed to give me what I was looking for.

This being so, I stopped going to them and decided to seek out a wise and experienced man who would explain this mystery to me, seeing that my spirit was inescapably drawn to it.

I searched for a long time : I would read the Bible, and wonder whether somewhere there might not exist some master of the spiritual life who could serve me as a wise and experienced guide.

I took to the road once more, without really knowing where to go.

I was depressed by my failure to find what I was looking for, and to console myself, I would read the Bible. I had been walking like this along a main road for five days, when one evening I met a little old man who looked like a religious. In response to my question, he said he was a monk who lived as a hermit, along with some other brothers, some ten kilometres away, and he invited me to stay with him.

'At our house,' he said, 'we receive pilgrims, we attend to their needs and offer them shelter.'

I was not too keen to go with him, and replied : 'My peace of mind does not depend on my being housed, but on spiritual instruction; I am not looking for food, since I have plenty of dry bread in my sack.'

'But what kind of instruction are you looking for, and what is it you want to understand? Do come with me, brother. We have some experienced *staretz* who could give you spiritual direction, and set you on the right path in the light of the word of God and the teachings of the Fathers.'

'But look, Father, it is about a year now since I heard the apostle's injunction, "pray constantly", during the Divine Office. Not knowing how the phrase was to be understood, I set about reading the Bible. And there too I found many passages containing God's command that we should pray constantly, in all circumstances, in all places, not only in the course of our daily work, but while we are asleep as well : "I sleep, but my heart is awake."

'This struck me very forcibly; I could not see how such a thing was possible, nor the means to achieve it. Such violent longing and feelings of curiosity were roused within me that the words did not leave my mind, day or night.

'From then on I became restless and unsure of myself.'

The *staretz* made the sign of the cross and began to speak. 'Thank God, my brother, who has filled you with this irresis-

tible attraction towards constant interior prayer. Recognize it
as the call of God, and find your peace once again in the
thought that the response of your will to the word of God has
been severely tested.

'God himself had enabled you to grasp this, and it will certainly not be thanks to any worldly wisdom or desire based on
empty curiosity that you will reach the heavenly light of interior prayer. On the contrary, it will be through poverty of
spirit, simplicity of heart, and actual experience.

'You should not be surprised that you have heard nothing
profound about the act of prayer itself; that no one has taught
you how to achieve this constant activity of the soul.

'In fact people preach a great deal about prayer, and there
are many recent books on the subject, but the authors' arguments are almost always based on intellectual speculation, on
rational principles, and almost never on the actual experience
of prayer nourished by deeds. More is said about the attributes of prayer than about its essence. One man will tell you
precisely why it is necessary to pray; another will illustrate for
you the power and the advantages of prayer; a third will describe the conditions that are necessary in order to pray well,
the attentiveness, devotion and purity of soul that are required, and so on and so on.

'But what prayer is and how one learns to pray – questions
which are fundamental – preachers rarely tell you these days,
because they involve something far more demanding than all
their arguments, and require not so much academic knowledge
as mystical understanding.

'And the sad thing is that only too often their superficial
human wisdom leads them to judge God by human standards.
Many make the mistake of thinking that it is the methods and
the good actions which produce the prayer, whereas in reality
prayer is the source of all virtues and all good works.

'They wrongly take the fruits and outward effects of prayer
to be the means of achieving it, and in so doing diminish its

power. This is a point of view entirely contrary to the passage in Scripture, where St Paul says : "First of all, I urge you to pray" (1 Tm 2 : 1). Many good works are demanded of the Christian, but the work of prayer ranks above all because without it no other good can be achieved.

'Without frequent prayer, one cannot find the way that leads to the Lord, nor can one know the Truth, crucify the flesh with its unruly passions, or be inwardly enlightened by the light of Christ and unite oneself to him in the work of salvation.'

Continuing our conversation in this way, we had without realising it made our way to the little monastery. In order, therefore, not to leave the wise old man before I had satisfied my desire to learn, I said quickly : 'Please, reverend father, *you* explain to me what constant interior prayer is about and what one must do to achieve it. I can see that your experience is deep and genuine.'

The *staretz* granted my request and invited me in.

'Come with me, and I will give you a book of the writings of the Fathers which will help you to understand clearly what prayer is, to learn to practise it with the help of God.'

We entered his cell, and the *staretz* addressed me with these words : 'The interior and constant practice of the Jesus prayer involves a continuous, uninterrupted invocation of the name of Jesus with the lips, with the heart and with the understanding, together with awareness of his presence at all times and, in all places, even during one's sleep. It is expressed in the words : Lord Jesus, Christ, have mercy on me !

'Anyone who makes habitual use of this invocation experiences great consolation as a result, and feels the need to repeat it over and over again. After a while, he cannot do without it, to such an extent that he hears it repeated within him without his having spoken it with his lips.

'Now do you understand what constant prayer is?'

'I understand perfectly, father,' I cried, full of joy, 'but now, in the name of God, teach me how I can reach this state myself.'

'We will discover together in this book how one learns to pray. It is called the *Philocalia*, and it contains fully detailed teaching, elaborated by the Fathers, on interior prayer. It is such a useful and perfect book that it is considered to be an essential guide to the contemplative life.'

So the *staretz* opened the *Philocalia*, chose a passage from St Simeon, and began to read : 'Remain seated, in silence and alone; bow your head, close your eyes, and breathe gently; try to direct your imagination and thought processes to within your heart; and as you breathe in and out say : Lord Jesus Christ, have mercy on me, in a low voice, or even simply interiorly. Try to drive all other thoughts away, and repeat this exercise frequently.'

I listened, attentive and wondering, trying to memorize all that the *staretz* was saying to me. We passed the entire night away in this way, and went at dawn to recite matins without having slept at all.

As he said goodbye, the *staretz* blessed me and told me to come back to him in the course of my study of prayer.

In church, I felt within me a burning zeal which impelled me to study this constant interior prayer with great care, and I begged God to help me.

Then I went in search of somewhere to live, since I could not stay in the convent guest rooms for more than three days.

Fortunately I knew of some lodgings only four miles away. I went to find a place there and God helped me. I offered my services as watchman to a farmer, in return for being allowed to spend the summer alone in a hut at the bottom of the garden.

Thanks be to God, I had found a really peaceful spot. It was there that, using the method I had been shown, I set about practising and learning more about interior prayer, going from time to time to visit my *staretz*. For a full week, in my garden solitude, I worked hard at my study of interior prayer,

following exactly my *staretz*'s advice. At first everything seemed to go well. Then I began to experience a great sense of
weariness. Boredom, laziness and an unbearable desire to sleep
descended on me like heavy clouds.

Full of misgivings, therefore, I went back to the *staretz* and
described my condition to him.

He received me kindly, and said :

'My brother, what you are experiencing is the war the
powers of evil have declared on you – for the world fears
nothing more than the prayer of the heart. Satan tries to make
things difficult for you, and to give you a distaste for prayer.
Your humility must still be put to the test, for it is too early
as yet to attain something so sublime.

'Here are some beads with which you can begin to recite
three thousand invocations a day. Standing or sitting, lying
down or walking, keep repeating to yourself : Lord Jesus Christ,
have mercy on me. Say it softly, without hurrying. This is how
you will arrive at that uninterrupted activity of the heart.'

Joyfully I took in what the *staretz* said, and made my way
back to my hut. Exactly and faithfully, I begun to put what
I had heard into practice. I had some further difficulty for a
couple of days, then it all became so simple that when I was
not repeating the prayer, I felt the need to start saying it
again, and it ebbed and flowed within me easily and gently,
with none of the tension of the first few days.

I told the *staretz* about this, and he commanded me to
repeat it six thousand times each day, adding, 'Don't be anxious about it, and try to be faithful to what I have recommend-
ed. God will have mercy on you.'

All that week, I kept to the seclusion of my hut, reciting
the six thousand invocations each day and not worrying
about anything else or wrestling with my own thoughts : I
simply tried to carry out exactly the precepts of my *staretz*.

What happened?

I became so accustomed to praying that if I stopped, even

for a moment, I experienced a sense of emptiness, as if I had lost something. But as soon as I started again I became light-hearted and happy once more.

I wanted to remain there alone – I had no desire to see anyone, and I was completely happy.

When I went back to the *staretz* I described this joy to him, and after he had listened to me he said : 'Now that you have made a habit of prayer, try to maintain that habit, and strengthen it. Never waste time, love solitude, rise early, and resolve to remain united to God.'

One morning early, I was, as it were, woken up by prayer. I began to say my morning prayers, but it was as if my tongue was tied, and I was overcome with the desire simply to repeat the Jesus Prayer. I began to repeat it and was immediately happy. My lips moved effortlessly, of their own accord.

I passed the whole of that day in a state of joy. It was as though I was detached from everything, and I felt as if I was in another world. I went to see the *staretz* and gave him a detailed account of all this. When I had finished, he said : 'God has given you the desire to pray, and the capacity to do so without effort.

'What heights of perfection, what ecstatic joy, man can experience, when the Lord wishes to reveal the secrets of prayer to him and purify his passions ! It is an indescribable state, and the revelation of this mystery is like a foretaste of the delights of heaven. This is the gift which they receive who seek the Lord with love and with singleness of heart.

'Now you can recite as many prayers as you wish. Invoke the name of Jesus without bothering to count, and comply humbly with the will of God, trusting in his help. He will not abandon you, and will guide you on your way.'

From then on, how happy I was ! What joy to feel within me the fervour of my prayer. Whenever I went into a church, I burned with love for Jesus.

My solitary hut seemed like a magnificent palace, and I did

not know how to thank God for having such an excellent *staretz* to a poor sinner like myself.

But unfortunately I had not much longer to take advantage of his direction : my beloved master died at the end of the summer. Weeping, I took leave of him, and thanking him for his teaching I asked him to leave me, by way of a blessing, the beads he always used to pray with.

And so I found myself alone once more.

The summer came to an end and the garden produce was gathered in. The farmer gave me two silver roubles in payment. I filled my knapsack with bread for the journey and went back to my wandering life.

But I was no longer poor, as I had been previously. Invoking the name of Jesus made my travelling a joyous affair, and everywhere I met with kindness. It seemed that everyone was predisposed to love me.

So here I am on the road once more, constantly reciting the Jesus Prayer which is dearer and more precious to me than anything else. Often I cover more than seventy kilometres a day, and I have no idea where I am going. When the cold bites into me I recite the prayer more attentively, and immediately I feel warmer.

If my hunger becomes too acute, I call on the name of Jesus more frequently and forget that I am hungry.

If I feel ill, or if my legs or my back ache, I concentrate on the prayer and the pain passes.

If anyone offends me, I think of nothing but the sweet Jesus Prayer, and immediately the anger or hurt disappears, and I forget all about it. I have become a bit strange.

I no longer get anxious about anything. External realities have no hold on me. My only wish is to remain alone and pray continually; then I am completely happy.

God knows what has taken place within me; I do not. I only know that I am happy, and that I now understand what the Apostle meant when he said : 'Pray constantly.'

Chapter Eight

UNLESS YOU CHANGE AND BECOME
LIKE LITTLE CHILDREN . . .

I have re-read that *Story of a Russian Pilgrim* many times, not merely because it is an authentic mystical text of great purity, but also because from it, as well as from other texts of the same kind, I have gleaned solid supporting material for my own attraction to spiritual childhood. The more involved I have found myself in the world of culture, or large scale concerns, or specialization, the more have I needed to simplify my spiritual life; the more contact I have with Christians with intellectual problems, the more I have tried to safeguard my prayer behind the curtain of lowliness and wisdom of heart. I must admit that, at the end – or nearly – of my journey, I am more attracted by the gentleness of a Pope John, the simplicity of a Père de Foucauld, than by any of the learned observations that have been spoken or written for or against *aggiornamento* in the Church.

I have too often been wounded by 'intelligent' people, disconcerted by unloving champions of orthodoxy or by self-advertising revolutionaries who are incapable of an act of humility.

Wishing to protect my poor soul from the babble of useless talk, I took up once more the simple rosary that my mother had wanted me to recite daily when I was boy.

Either I have seen too much of life, or else I have witnessed too many failures. One thing, however, is certain : that I put more and more faith in the simplicity of the Gospel, and I can appreciate the concern of Christ when he said to his friends : 'Unless you change and become like little children, you will never enter the kingdom of heaven.'

To become like children is not easy for men as riddled with pride as we are; that is why Jesus warned us so uncompromisingly : 'You will never enter !'

I realize that no one will believe me, but I have no hesitation about affirming that a serious beginning is made in the spiritual life the moment a man makes a genuine act of humility. So often for most men the early stages of faith, or, in the case of others its development, is blocked, poisoned, distorted, or relegated to an everlasting tomorrow by our inability to become like a child and to cast ourselves, in the spirit of a child, into the enfolding arms of God's mystery. We try to show God how clever we are, when no class of men is so abhorrent to the Gospel; we want to lay down conditions to the Eternal and Infinite One, but the Infinite does not respond, and the Eternal allows time to destroy us.

This is why I loved and still love that young pilgrim : he has the heart of a child and does not lay down conditions to his God.

So God taught him to pray, and God took him up into his own peace and joy, in spite of his dreadful poverty and his unrelieved sufferings. Although he does not realize it himself, he has undoubtedly reached the end of the journey of prayer : he has become a living prayer. He lives in a state of pure prayer, in a union with God so complete that it recalls the extraordinary experience of St Benedict Joseph Labré who travelled as a pilgrim along the roads that lead from France to the holy places in Rome.

Purified by trials, immersed in the purifying waters of evangelical poverty, detached from material things, the young man became an empty vessel filled by the Spirit of God, a musical instrument, ready and waiting to be played by the supraterrestrial hand that is capable of drawing from it celestial harmonies.

Yet he reached these heights by making use of the simplest means imaginable.

A single phrase, repeated like a single, uninterrupted note, acceptance of the events of daily life as part of the mystery of Providence, a Bible in his knapsack, and a bit of dry bread.

We westerners, who consider ourselves to be so experienced in theological matters, smile condescendingly at such a childish method of prayer – so mechanical, so naive!

Have we never smiled at the rosaries of our grandmothers?

But the fact of the matter is that this young man has passed through the wall that separates us from the invisible, and our elders were contemplatives without realizing it, while we, rich in our thoughts and man-made securities, run the risk of dying of subastral cold, far from Jesus, the Sun of our universe.

For it was Jesus himself who said, in a moment of spiritual exhilaration: 'I bless you, Father, Lord of heaven and of earth, for hiding these things from the learned and the clever and revealing them to mere children' (Mt 11 : 25).

And this is the first thing we must keep in mind as we enter the school of prayer.

The Father reveals himself to little ones; the Father hides himself from the learned.

This is not a joke!

If we want to know God, to become close friends of the Most High, we must acquire the habit of contemplative prayer, made with the eyes of humility and with simplicity of heart.

Yes, to become lowly, lowlier still – as lowly as possible. This is the great secret of the mystical life. And then, having reduced oneself to a single point and become nothing more than a soul which watches attentively and a heart which loves, to get used to a complete reversal of the usual position – the eternal position of pride, and the uneasy position of the ego which always sees itself as the centre of the universe.

At this point let us call to mind one very important thing :

prayer is not so much a matter of talking as listening; contemplation is not watching but being watched.

On the day when we realize this, we will have entered finally into possession of the truth, and prayer will have become a living reality. To be watched by God : that is how I would define contemplation, which is passive rather than active, more a matter of silence than of words, of waiting rather than of action.

What am I before God?

What can I do to be worthy of his revelation?

If he shuts, no one opens, and if he opens, no one shuts. He is the active principle of love, he is before all, he is the one who makes within me his own prayer, which then becomes my prayer.

I do not know what has happened or is happening within you, but I do know what has happened and is happening within myself, and I can tell you this : that it was he who sought me in the first place, and it is he who continues to seek me.

At first it was more difficult to recognize his presence, to feel the movement of his hand, but now that I have *experienced him* it has become easier, even though the locus of encounter between him and myself is darker and the memory of that experience harder to capture. With God I have never had great difficulties in the area of faith and I can only say that in spite of my infidelities, my sins, my egoism, and my superficiality, there is no longer any creature – star or flower, meadow or hill, storm wind or fine weather, ocean or bird – which does not speak to me of him, which is not a message and a symbol, a word and a warning from him. I feel I am in him like a bee in its hive, like a bride in her own home, or, better still, like a child in its mother's womb. This last comparison is the most faithful I have found because it says, in a very real way, that union with God is not something that has to be found because it already 'is', just as the union between the mother and her infant already 'is'. At the most it is a question of becoming aware of it; of fostering it through our adherence to him; of responding to his incessant calls, because in God 'we live and move and have our being' (St Paul).

But it is not only that. To say that we are in God like a child in the womb of its mother is to draw attention (given that comparisons are never quite perfect) to the inequalities that exist in the relationship of the two – between the possibilities, the attentiveness, the awareness and the love of the mother, and the helplessness, smallness, blindness and passivity of the child. Our relationship with God is even more unequal than this. Our blindness is greater than that of the foetus. Our possibilities are even more circumscribed. I am not exaggerating. Look around and see how some great men have ended up, how some dictators have oppressed their people. If their places had been taken by children, fewer disasters would have befallen us. And each one of us could produce endless examples from his own experience to bear out what Christ affirmed in the Gospel : *without me you can do nothing.* And nothing means nothing. Let that much at least be understood.

But if Jesus needed to tell us that without him we could do nothing, his implication was : *but with me you can do all things.*

This is one of the paradoxical results of our union with God : the omnipotence of impotence, the knowledge of ignorance, the courage of weakness – all expressed in the cry of St Paul : *If Christ is with me, who can be against me?*

The child in the womb of God means peace in the midst of the storm, security amid the trial of life, light in the darkness, hope in the face of death.

What matters is that one should let oneself go, live by faith, trust in the Eternal – and above all understand one thing : that our growth depends on laws that are not of our own making, on a will that is more powerful than ours.

What can a child do in its mother's womb but wait, be patient, be still? One of the parables describes well this truth about the unfolding of the kingdom of God in an almost imperceptible manner. It is Mark who recounts it.

'He also said, "This is what the kingdom of God is like. A man throws seed on the land. Night and day, while he sleeps, when he is awake, the seed is sprouting and growing; how, he does not know" ' (Mk 4 :25). Nor do we know how, but to accept that he brings it about *without our knowing how* is a hard lesson to learn, and it takes us a long time to learn it by heart.

But when we have learned it, what joy we experience. To be able to live in the knowledge that God works while I am sleeping, thinks of me while I work or pray, and will intervene at the appropriate moment, that God awaits me in prayer, and knows my future.

This is true peace, the foretaste of heaven, and the answer to all my problems about faith.

Chapter Nine

PRAYER AND REVELATION

I said just now that contemplation is not so much a matter of watching God as of *being watched by God*. This is something I have learned by praying.

What do you want me to look at while I am praying? I can assure you that never do I feel so short-sighted as I do when I try to focus my eyes of God.

I would say that it is precisely in prayer that you learn to recognize more clearly than ever your own limitations, your measure as a created, not a creating being, the radical power-lessness of your poverty. And you will experience this above all if you have the courage to make your way in faith to *the frontiers of the invisible*.

When you have passed beyond the stages where sentiments, hymns, preoccupation with your own salvation, immediate results and easy achievements matter, and have reached the realm of mystery, then you understand what this world is.

When you have grown tired of setting up little altars on which to erect images of God, the product of your own fantasy, or worse, your theorizing, or, worst of all, your fears, and you reach the arid sands that separate the finite from the infinite, time from eternity, you have little left to think or say.

And then you realize that if contemplation were to depend on you, it would be a pretty sad, impoverished affair.

Emptied of its creative and imaginative powers, bowed and broken by suffering and dissatisfaction, your being would be able to utter no more than an anguished cry, and contemplation would simply mean staring at a grey horizon under northern skies, in an endless winter.

But through the grace of God, contemplation – true contemplation – does not depend on you. You are not the dawn, you are the land that awaits the dawn.

Your God is the dawn, and later he is full daylight, and later still high noon.

You are the land that waits for the light, the blackboard that waits for the white chalk of the draftsman who walks towards you with that chalk in his hand. Sit down and try to be still; sit still and try to hope. Leave behind you time, space, number, thought, reason, culture, and look ahead.

Look beyond yourself, beyond your helplessness and your limitations, and wait.

Your heart has been tried by suffering and darkness; now allow it to stop relying on the earth it is leaving.

Let your tears flow, to water the arid land of your faith. Persevere.

Do not think of anything else. God is before you.

God is coming to you.

Contemplation is not a matter of watching, but of being watched, and he is there watching you.

And if he is watching you, he loves you, and in loving you, he gives you what you are looking for : himself.

What other gift could there be for one who had searched so hard.

Our heart is so hard to satisfy.

God alone can fill it.

Things never can.

Yes, God is there before you, watching you.

His look is creative, capable of achieving the impossible.

And just as he looked on the chaos at the beginning, hovered over the waters with the smile of his favour, and drew forth the cosmos, so, looking at you with the same favouring smile, he realizes the final purpose of creation : love.

Take courage, then : God loves you.

I know you do not deserve it, so it is useless to go on saying so : the fact is he loves you.

I know you are tormented by doubts, but do not be afraid. He loves you, and his love is freely given. He does not love you for what you are worth; he loves you because, as God, he cannot help loving you : he is love.

Let yourself go; let him take hold of you.

He accepts you as a son.

I realize that you have fled so many times, that you have preferred strange countries to your own home, but all *that* belongs to the past, so stop thinking about it. The time has come for you to love.

But how can I love someone I do not know, respond to the love of someone I cannot see? I have been told that God is unknowable, and that is what makes the relationship so difficult.

You are right : God is unknowable, but being love, he has decided to make himself known.

Just as God, invisible and intangible, has made himself visible and tangible in Christ – has brought about the incarnation – so, in the same way, incommunicable and unknowable, he has become knowable and communicable through love.

By receiving his love in prayer, you enable him to make you the gift of knowledge of himself; by offering him the clean slate of your soul, you make it possible for him to trace on it the features of his own face. The unknowable becomes known; love crosses over the frontier of the invisible; the *beyond* crosses over onto this side, and becomes life. Jesus has described it as eternal life, defining exactly what he meant in the wonderful words, 'Eternal life is this : to know you, the only true God, and Jesus Christ whom you have sent' (Jn 17 : 3).

Union with God depends on knowledge and love : it is a vital reality.

And so, at last, we arrrive at the crux of the matter – the revelation of the mystery kept hidden for centuries, and revealed to us by Jesus in the fulness of time; the completion of the work of creation itself; the profound inner significance of the passion of Christ; the reason for the presence of the Holy Spirit within each one of us.

It is a question, no less, of bringing about the union of creature and creator, of the Father, who is God, with the son, ourselves. And since, as we have already said, this union is not juridical, but a real and vital union, it involves man's entry into the divine life, the divine life which Jesus defined above all as knowledge.

I cannot love what I do not know, and God, who understands this better than I do, cannot ask us to love him – or better, oblige us to love him with the first commandment : *You must love God above all things* – without first making sure that it is possible for us to know him.

This is not what I would call natural knowledge of God, analogical knowledge, which I can achieve by using my own reason or common sense. It is true supernatural knowledge, the same knowledge, that is, that I shall have when the veil of faith is torn aside and I see God face to face. Only God can give me this sort of knowledge, because only God can tell me 'what he is'.

Simply by assembling every conceivable human argument on the subject of God, I will not succeed in adding one centimetre to my height; but by accepting his revelation I enter immediately into the mystery, I become a member of his family, I live his same life.

These are the things that people ought to be saying in church, instead of wasting time criticizing the capitalists who are not present, or turning the Gospel into a sociological text (one hundred years late) on the message of Marx.

The true measure of the Christian is the divine life within him. His primary concern is that he should know God because such knowledge will bring with it the love of charity, which, as St Paul says, is a good surpassing all others, since it is God himself within you.

If I presume too much in saying these things and in believing them from the depths of my heart, the fault lies with Christ. It was he who said to me in the Gospel: 'I will will reveal myself to him' (Jn 14 : 21), and I promise you, that I have prayed for this revelation, I have waited for it, and longed for it with an almost unbearable longing.

And here on this arid meeting ground of the visible and invisible, ignorance of God and the possibility of knowing and loving him, I have played all the cards in my hand.

I have not been disappointed, and should you ask me why I believe in God, I would reply, 'because he has revealed himself to me' and should you ask what is the surest proof I have that I know him, I would reply, 'the fact that I have been with him'. St Thomas's five proofs for the existence of God have been a help to me, but the experience I have had of him in prayer helps me far more, and that is the only evidence I would produce for those of my brothers who are searching.

I am aware that in so saying, I am challenging them to set out on a journey through the desert, to renounce themselves totally, to give themselves to the Absolute; but I also know that the prize makes the hardness of the choice worth while, and what is more I know, as St Paul says, 'in whom I have believed'.

Do not be afraid. Listen to what someone who has already travelled this road has to say, my beloved Angela of Foligno:

'The soul, in the presence of God, is surrounded by darkness, and in that darkness comes to a knowledge of him which is greater than any I could have ever imagined was possible, and so splendid, so certain, so profound, that no heart could possibly invent or understand such a thing in any way at all.

'The soul can say absolutely nothing at all, because there are no words in which she can speak about it and express herself. Indeed, there is no thought or intelligence that can encompass such a thing, so far is it above all other things – just as God cannot be explained in terms of anything else that exists. When I turned the matter over in my mind, I knew with absolute certainty that those who are the most aware of God are the least able to talk about him.

'Precisely because they experience something of that infinite and ineffable good, they are less able to speak about it. May God grant that you remember this when you go to preach. For then you will be at a loss for anything to say about God; at which point anyone else might keep silent, but I would come up to you and say: Go on, brother, speak to me for a while about God.

'And you would be so overcome by the goodness of God, that you would be unable to say anything about him.

'And yet the soul does not lose consciousness, nor does the body lose contact with any of the senses; indeed, consciousness is entire within us.

'But you will say emphatically to the people: Go with the blessing of God, because I can say nothing at all!

'And I realize that everything that has been said in Scripture, and by all men from the beginning of the world up till the present moment seems capable of expressing virtually nothing about the heart of the matter, not even so much as a grain of sand in comparison with the universe.'

As for Angela of Foligno, so for us all. We are aware that the knowledge of God increases within us in the measure that our love for him increases.

But we can say nothing about this knowledge. We realize that it is, as theology tells us, an exquisite, mysterious, personal and dark knowledge of God, but we cannot say a word more about it.

This revelation of himself which God makes to man is the body and soul of so-called contemplative prayer, its breath of life, and it constitutes a genuine participation in eternal life.

'And eternal life is this : to know you, the only true God, and Jesus Christ whom you have sent' (Jn 17 : 3).

But what really matters in all this is the fact that the barrier created by our innate inability to advance in the knowledge of God can be overcome. There is one thing we can do; and it is, so to speak, within our reach : the possibility of loving.

The anonymous author of *The Cloud of Unknowing* says : 'Every intelligent creature, angel or man, has within him two principal faculties : one is called a faculty for knowing, the other a faculty for loving. God is the creator of both, but if, through the former, he remains incomprehensible, he can be perceived through the latter, according to each one's different ability. In this fashion, only the being who loves can, by virtue of his love, perceive him who is sufficient to the full to satiate all the souls and angels of creation.'

And the inexhaustible wonder, the miracle of love, is this : that our practice of it will never be interrupted because God ceaselessly rekindles it. And why? Because, since he can be loved but not thought, love can grasp and hold him; thought never can.

Which means that in the last analysis there exists within us a certain capacity to influence God, to approach God, to clasp him to ourselves : the power, that is, of loving. By loving one can achieve what is impossible through other means; by loving one can find God. This, fundamentally, is the sum and substance of all history, of our own history.

Let us keep this truth before us.

You say you have no faith? Love – and faith will come.

You say you are sad? Love – and joy will come.

You say you are alone? Love – and you will break out of your solitude.

You say you are in hell? Love – and you will find yourself in heaven. Heaven is love.

Chapter Ten

PRAYER AND LIFE

Life and prayer are inseparable.

A life without prayer is a life which fails to acknowledge the essential dimension of existence; it is a life which remains satisfied with what it sees, without discovering the grandeur, the eternal aspect of human destiny.

To plumb the depths of prayer is to discover, affirm and live the fact that everything has this vast, eternal dimension.

The world in which we live is not a profane world, even though we ourselves frequently succeed in profaning it. In itself it came from the hands of God, and is loved by God.

In order to appreciate the value God attributes to this world, it is sufficient to think of the life and death of his only Son. But that is something we come to understand as we pray, just as it is only by praying that we come to appreciate that everything around us has a sacred value in the eyes of God.

Not to pray is to exclude God from one's life, and not only God, but everything that he can signify in the world he created and in which we live.

If we want to learn to pray, we must first of all identify ourselves with every aspect of human reality, with man's destiny and that of the world. We must accept it in its entirety. This, basically, is the essential act which God accomplished in the Incarnation, and which became intercession on our behalf.

Normally speaking, when we think of intercession, we believe it to consist in respectfully reminding God of the things he has forgotten to do. In reality, intercession involves the taking of a step which brings us straight to the heart of a tragic situation; and, as Anthony Bloom points out, it is a step of the same quality as that taken by Christ, who became man once and for all.

We ourselves, as far as the world is concerned, must take the step that will lead us to the heart of a situation from which we must never seek to withdraw.

It is not easy, but the trouble is that we have a mistaken idea of life, just as we have of prayer.

Only too often we imagine that life consists in being immensely active, while prayer consists in withdrawing to some place apart, completely forgetting about our neighbour and our human situation. This is quite wrong : it is a misrepresentation of life and a misrepresentation of prayer as well.

If there are moments or longer periods of time when, in order to establish a personal relationship with God, we create a solitude within ourselves, a temporary state of withdrawal, we do so knowing that he will himself remind us of our fellow men and send us back to them, in order that, together with them, we should give concrete expression to our love.

It is God himself, incarnate in Christ – the most sublime and most vital manifestation of love – who has given to each one of us and to his Church, as his own commandment, the commandment of fraternal love : 'Love one another as I have loved you.' To the extent, that is, of total self-sacrifice.

But let us begin at the beginning. Learning to pray means, above all, identifying oneself with every aspect of earthly existence. Anyone who prays to God must be, or endeavour to become, one who looks on the whole of creation with a sympathetic eye – on all reality, physical and spiritual; on nature and on grace; on the rocks on which he places his feet, and on the angels in whom he believes on the testimony of Christ and who inhabit the invisible world. As long as man is unable to accept creation, he will be unable to enter into a relationship of love with the God who fashioned and sustains it, and who continues to fashion and sustain what he has created.

The whole is a unity, and God is at the heart of this unity.

God is like the face of reality, the heart of the universe, and until I can look on created things with sympathy and understanding, I will not be able to enter into vital communication with the One who willed both my existence and that of the entire universe.

To believe that God is present in my prayer means making room within it for the fulness of his thought, his will, which has been realized and is being realized in creation.

Obviously I may come into contact with things I do not understand, and have to accept through faith, but I cannot begin to pray if I put a question mark over everything and remain for ever on the threshold of faith.

I can say, 'I do not understand this yet, but God will explain it to me in his own good time', but in order to pray, I must begin to say 'Our Father, who art in heaven', which means making a first genuinely serious gesture of optimism.

By saying 'Father', I say a thousand and one important things; and I say above all, 'I am beginning to trust you because you are a father and a father could not betray my hopes.'

You are a father who is hidden from us, but you are still a father, and from now on I can greet you with confidence, even though many things still remain a mystery to me.

A woman who belonged to a society for the protection of animals once said to me : 'I will never be able to believe in God as long as I see animals suffering, and as long as butchers continue to exist.'

I appreciate this woman's confusion – it is certainly a strange thing to watch a cat mauling a bird and to realize that in the created order everything lives at the expense of someone or something else; but if I stop there I will not penetrate very far into the mystery, and my own death will overtake me while I am standing there thinking, without understanding, about the deaths of calves in the slaughterhouses of Paris or Bologna. If the idea of the slaughterhouse was holding this good lady back from God, she should realize that the whole universe is one vast slaughterhouse, and it is not only cattle who pay the price for this.

Yet what do we know about what happens in the heaven of slaughtered creatures? What happens when a gazelle dies, or a rabbit parts with its flesh in the hands of the housewife?

We know nothing, or virtually nothing, and yet we presume to pass judgment on everything. We are like children who say to the doctor who prescribes our medicine, 'bad doctor'!

What I am saying may seem trivial, but it is just such trivial matters as these which keep many people back from a serious life of prayer. They deny themselves the possibility of communication with God simply because they have not yet been able to face the fact that the fire which burns and the knife which cuts the flesh are part of life.

Each one of us is entitled to outline the plan or plans according to which he, in his wisdom, would have created the universe. I believe, however, that on the day when we see God face to face – the day, that is, when things are revealed to us as they are – if those plans still lie hidden in our pockets, we will hurriedly destroy them in disgust as we are faced at last with the truth : 'What a fool you have been! Is there no limit to your self-importance?'

And this will be a good beginning for our entry into eternal life.

Having accepted God's plan for ourselves and the world, we should at least desire to put it into practice.

I say 'desire' because putting it into effect is not always

easy. Many people accept in theory that it is more logical, more sincere, more in keeping with the nature of love to have one wife, but at the same time they are few who conform to this plan.

And yet the plan is clear enough.

There is a design in creation which is visible enough, even to the naked eye. And it is visible, furthermore, because within our conscious minds the Creator of all things has left a model, as it were, a chart which can help us to discover the truth, and a compass to enable us to find our bearings on the chart without getting lost.

And yet . . .

An elderly doctor, who had an exaggerated fear of death, used to say to me, 'If only I had your faith, Brother Carlo! What comfort it would bring me! It is obvious that you are at peace, at one with yourself. But what should I do? I have no faith, and I cannot give it to myself.'

The old doctor used to repeat this little speech for my benefit rather too frequently, and as in the end I had the impression that he was using it to justify himself, thus taking refuge in unreality, I once said to him, 'Doctor, do you really want to have faith? Do you want to die at peace with God and men?

'Well then, let the servant whom you keep as a mistress leave the house. You know quite well that she is poor and only agrees to sleep with you because of her poverty. Make her a small settlement, and then let her go off and start a family.

'Rediscover the friendship and compassionate understanding of your wife, sell your estate and distribute the proceeds to the poor, extricate yourself from your appalling egoism, look at people optimistically and stop saying they are evil . . . then you will see.

'Trust me in what I say. Put your house in order, and within a year you will see your faith grow great like an oak tree, and all your doubts disappear.'

In all this I was wrong about only one thing – the date.

Not a year, but a few days after his decision, he had come to the Eucharist. I realize I am carrying coals to Newcastle in saying all this, but let me insist.

So often our prayer lights upon the right path, uncovers the gushing stream, at the moment when we take a step forward in accepting the will of God, whatever it might be, and at whatever stage it happens to find us.

There is a close link between prayer and life : we frequently look on them as unconnected realities, then we see them as drawing closer together, but by the end of our lives we must see them as a single reality. To pray is to live, and living becomes prayer.

There is something else that needs to be said about the connection between life and prayer, a deeply significant, indeed a divine truth, since it was Jesus himself who said it : 'A man can have no greater love than to lay down his life for his friends' (Jn 15 : 13).

One must transform one's own life into an act of self-giving. From then on it becomes 'prayer' and I suddenly achieve the synthesis, the unity of my being, and I break through into the real.

He who becomes a gift, is in a state of perfection; he becomes invulnerable, he is light.

To be a gift to God, a gift to one's fellow men.

The union of these two elements is what makes the Christian, the authentic human being, the saint.

People today are fond of the expression : make yourself available, and it makes a good beginning.

But one needs to go further than that, even if it is terribly difficult and demanding; one needs to become a gift. A gift is something permanent, something previously offered and therefore not open to question, whereas we are so fond of questioning everything.

A gift is an expression of love, but we are more attracted

by the truth because it is more manageable, easier to grasp.

And moreover . . . each one of us sees his own truth.

And since it often happens that the man standing next to me sees a different one, the clashes begin.

The origin of all wars lies in this separation of truth and love.

That is why it is better to become a 'gift' because the gift is more likely to bring peace – which cannot always be said of that which we call 'truth'.

Had Jesus been satisfied with being Truth, and not become a gift, we would still need to be saved. If, having proclaimed the truth to man, he had claimed their immediate consent to it, we would be in hell. It was precisely when no one believed him that he kept silent and allowed himself to be killed. But in dying he became a gift, and so he saved us.

We must learn from him how and to what extent one can interpret the truth, but above all we must let him teach us when the only thing to do is to keep silence, and to go to the depths in love.

And not to make judgments at such moments.

Above all, not to strike out.

Anyone who strikes out when love and truth are not at one within him, misdirects his blows, and the results are invariably disastrous.

The same applies to the slap a man gives 'in hate' to his own son, and to a papal bull which drives a section of the flock outside the Church. Anyone who does not love is in death, and death can only produce corpses, even when it is surrounded by all the truth in heaven an earth.

Chapter Eleven

AND THE NIGHT SHALL BE CLEAR AS THE DAY

I got up at three o'clock to pray.

Very quietly, so as not to wake the brethren, who were sleeping in the adjoining cells, I went out into the night.

I crossed the courtyard, and found myself in complete darkness.

There was a cold nip in the air, but I was sufficiently protected by my *burnous*.

I left the hermitage buildings behind me, and made for the nearby slope in order to watch the stars.

This, for me, is the best preparation for prayer.

Above my head, in all its magnificence, stretched the winter sky of Beni-Abbès.

The profound darkness resulting from the absence of the moon, which was in its last quarter, made it particularly easy to see the stars.

The constellation Leo was passing through the south-west, with its brilliant star Regulus. Virgo's ear of corn, with its unmistakable glow, dominated the Tropic; next came the Lynx, and then the Great Bear, which rose up in the eastern sky, drawing behind it the tail of the Dragon.

I always count it as something precious when, before embarking on my prayer, I am able to fill my gaze with the pure, mysterious light that comes from the stars.

Everyone has his own method, his own way of going about things. The important thing is to realize that it is difficult to reach the point when one can get down on one's knees immediately. We need some moments of preparation, a little time in which to calm the soul, or to wake it up – a vestige of human prudence, so as not to turn up like brutes for such an exacting task as prayer.

For me, the process of star-gazing was a great help.

Others help themselves by contemplating an arrangement of flowers, a meadow, a sunset, a lamb, the view of a sleeping city from an open window. Some focus their attention on the crucifix; others finger their rosary, thinking of one of the mysteries in the life of Our Lady. The important thing is that we should realize that we are little, and must help ourselves in little ways.

How hard we find it to keep our blessed psyche at peace – our complicated, tormented psyche!

And this wretched body which complains incessantly, which always has something wrong with it somewhere, which troubles one, clamours for attention and weighs one down – oh! what a tiresome burden it can be!

And there is nothing to be done about it : one must bear with the first and look after the second; one must be patient and not press too much; give a shake where necessary, but otherwise leave things as they are. No, it is not easy to establish oneself in a state of prayer, to find a bit of peace, relaxation and calm. There is always something in the way!

People really make me laugh when they say, 'You have to bring everything into your prayer, every aspect of yourself.' It is obvious that they are talking about prayer in the abstract, as one might talk about the polar ice-cap without ever having seen it, or about journeying across the desert when one has never so much as set eyes on a sand-dune. Bring everything? I can tell you I would like to bring nothing with me, to contrive, for an hour at least, to forget myself, my poor head, and my heart. To succeed in keeping my imagination in check, bundling it into some corner or other in order to be left in peace, just for that one hour.

And then there are those who come and tell you, with impressive arguments, that you must bring your fellow men with you, have them present continually.

'My God!' a telephonist once said to me, 'from morning till night I'm harassed by my neighbours, first at home, then in the office, and then in the course of my various social engagements. When can I find five minutes to be alone with God?' The telephonist was right, and not those who ramble on about prayer without ever having had any real experience of it. In order to pray, one needs a modicum of solitude, of detachment and withdrawal. This is what the desert, retreat, getting down on one's knees, is all about. One cannot spend all one's time with the community, otherwise one ends up denying that God is the Absolute. Do not be alarmed. I shall return to my brethren, of course, I shall. Jesus himself compels me to do so, though I assure you that, were it not for him, I would flee to the desert and never come back.

To all community enthusiasts I say : all right, I will give you twenty-three hours, but allow me to have the twenty-fourth alone with God.

To take prayer seriously means giving at least the twenty-fourth hour to God – and to God alone.

Simply because he is God, the Absolute.

He is entitled to expect that I should drop everything for him, just as the visitor who comes to see me has the right to expect it.

How reassuring it is to go into the house of friends, and watch everything stop because you have arrived.

We westerners, with all our rushing, have lost sight of this 'sacred' approach to the welcoming of guests. Here in the desert it still exists, as it did in the time of Abraham, and it is manifested in the most wonderful way. Listen to what the Bible has to say about the way visitors should be received :

'Yahweh appeared to him at the Oak of Mamre while he

was sitting by the entrance of the tent during the hottest part of the day. He looked up, and there he saw three men standing near him. As soon as he saw them he ran from the entrance of the tent to meet them, and bowed to the ground. "My lord," he said, "I beg you, if I find favour with you, kindly to not pass your servant by. A little water shall be brought; you shall wash your feet and lie down under the tree. Let me fetch a little bread and you shall refresh yourselves before going further. That is why you have come in your servant's direction." They replied, "Do as you say."

'Abraham hastened to the tent to find Sarah. "Hurry," he said, "knead three bushels of flour and make loaves." Then running to the cattle Abraham took a fine and tender calf and gave it to the servant, who hurried to prepare it. Then taking cream, milk and the calf he had prepared, he laid all before them, and they ate while he remained standing near them under the trees' (Gen 18 : 1–8).

What has always struck me about the way in which these simple men receive visitors is their ability to put all activity to one side. You, the guest, become the focal point, and they range themselves round you in a circle. If the owner of the tent has planned to go on a journey, he puts it off : now he must concern himself with you. If his wife was thinking of doing the laundry, she piles it all up on one side : now she must see about serving you.

The guest is sacred : everything else is less important.

For the time being you are the one who matters : time is less important. And if the visitor, who has left one corner of the world in order to search you out and spend a bit of time with you, has these rights, surely God has the same right, he who came from heaven itself to find you; who took flesh in order to become visible for you; who became the Eucharist in order to gain entrance to your tent and stay there as long as possible.

D

Here and only here, in fact, is to be found the meaning of prayer, the power that sustains it, and the hope that gives it life : there is one who seeks you, one who stands before you saying : 'Look, I am standing at the door, knocking. If one of you hears me calling and opens the door, I will come and share his meal, side by side with him' (Rv 3 :20). If prayer meant addressing oneself to a mute, unheeding wall, I guarantee the Bible would never have been written. I guarantee that the saints would have grown wise to the fact, and years ago the abbey of Monte Cassino, the monasteries of Mount Athos or in the Tibetan mountains would have fallen into ruin.

Prayer is meaningful because in your presence Another is present, another mouth corresponds to your mouth, another ear to your ear.

In this way it becomes something real, vital, authentic.

Under the impulse of this conviction I managed to get up in the night – and I can tell you it is not pleasant.

And it is filled with this hope that I now prepare myself for prayer. I go back down the slope and re-enter the hermitage. It is the same one that Père de Foucauld, thirsting for prayer, built for himself in this desert of Beni-Abbès.

The room, poor as any other, with walls of beaten clay and earthen floor covered by a layer of beautiful clean sand from the dunes, is of an extreme simplicity.

The bright flame of the sanctuary lamp, fed by the purest olive oil, flickers and casts its light into the semi-darkness.

I wrap my soul round with that light, and my body with the *burnous* which keeps me warm, and kneel down on the sand to pray.

You will ask me : why did you go back inside?

Could you not pray under the stars? Would it not have been easier?

Is not nature the principal reminder we have of Almighty God?

And you might even be right, but you must listen to my

explanation. There is no absolute law about praying in church. One can find God perfectly well out under the stars, or in the midst of the city crowds. We have all tried these things out ourselves. But . . .

There are three really important things in my life : the Cosmos, the Bible and the Eucharist.

I could pray outside under the stars, which represent the Cosmos for me; I could pray with the Bible, which is the Word of God; but if I can I prefer to pray before the Eucharist, which is the very presence of him for whom everything was created and who was revealed by the Bible as saviour of the world.

The Eucharist recapitulates the Cosmos for me; the Eucharist recapitulates the Bible for me. All three bear the divine within them, and all three are worthy to be there while I am praying, but the third is the greatest.

The Eucharist is the fulness of the gift, it is the pearl hidden in the mystery of Scripture, the treasure in the field of the Word of God, the secret of the King. In the Eucharist God becomes a presence beside me on my path, bread in my knapsack, friendship close to my heart as a man. To those who have not the courage to say there is nothing there and leave the tabernacle unattended; to those who behave as though there were no living presence there, I would say : assume that it *is* true; assume that under the sacramental sign there is the living presence of Jesus. Assume that the faith of the Church, which has always accepted this mystery of faith, is the authentic response to such a sublime reality; surely I am justified in coming to spend a bit more time here in his presence.

You will say : but the Eucharist was made to be eaten, Jesus said so himself. That is true, and I shall eat it tomorrow, and the day after tomorrow, and so on to the last day of my life; but between one meal and another, one *agape* and another, is Jesus absent from me? Has he given me his body and withheld himself? Has he given me his blood and denied me his friendship?

I need bread, but I assure you I feel the need of friendship quite as much, and nothing gives me the friendship of Jesus more than the Gospel and the Eucharist.

You will tell me I am old-fashioned to go on believing in visits to the Blessed Sacrament. Still, I *do* believe that Jesus is present in the Eucharist not only during the mass, but also between one mass and the next : always. And how helpful this belief has been to me; what great things this presence has given me!

It was here, before it, that I learned to pray.

When, in the desert, my novice master left me alone for eight days; when, later on, I remained alone in a hermitage for forty days, I would have gone mad had it not been for this presence answering to the needs of my presence, this love responding to the demands of my love.

It is here that I have felt the presence of God most strongly; it is here that I have experienced for myself Christ's dramatic recapitulation of the history of salvation.

And I always come back here when I want to make my way to the threshold of the invisible, because the Eucharist is the surest doorway opening on to it.

Here I am, then, alone before that door – or, rather, that window – which opens on to the invisible at the extreme limits of human reality. Faith alone is my guide, and I assure you that I know, both in my heart and in my flesh, what 'mystery of faith' means.

To find oneself confronted by a piece of bread, and to believe that it is the presence of Jesus, involves an act of faith : reason is inadequate.

But faith is bare, dark and frequently painful.

Once I get past the barrier of my feelings, however, and cast myself with confidence into the abyss of God, my faith is joined by hope, and love sustains me. Just as each of the three Divine Persons seeks the other two within the framework of the unity, so each of the theological virtues gathers to itself the other two theological virtues. And as soon as you succeed in holding them strongly within your grasp, keeping them united before you, you can fashion a sword sharp enough to cut through to the invisible.

The sign of bread both conceals and points to the presence of Jesus; faith, hope and charity cut through the barrier that separates me from him and reveal his presence. It is Jesus himself, Son of God and son of Mary, Jesus of Bethlehem, of Nazareth, of the Last Supper, of Calvary, Jesus of the Resurrection, yesterday, today and the same for ever.

Now leave me with him for a while – with him, who chose to come to me as bread so as not to overwhelm me. Let me contemplate his life and his Gospel, as told by the Eucharist.

This bread speaks to me of humility, of lowliness, of self-giving. It tells me the parable he invented to explain me and to explain himself, it epitomizes for me his preferences, which find in the bread the model and symbol dearest to him. Bread, not a stone; bread, not luxuries; bread, not arms; bread, not punishment; bread, not gold.

Above all, it tells me that it is with this bread – with which he became bread – that he will nourish me for eternal life. ' . . . anyone who eats this bread will live for ever' (Jn 6 :58).

But was it not for that reason that we started on our way : he towards us, and we towards him? Was it not to find some point of contact between heaven and earth that we persevered to the frontiers of the Eternal? to discover the *beyond* that we have left created realities behind us? And do I not place myself in the Father's presence to receive the gift of divine sonship? Yes, in the Father's presence, before Jesus, the window that opens on to the invisible.

For Jesus is the one who will enable me to see the Father and will speak to me of him.

Jesus is the One Who Reveals, in the fullest sense of that word. And in revealing himself he will reveal the Father to me : '. . . I shall . . . show myself to him' (Jn 14 : 21) in a supernatural revelation which is 'eternal life'. 'And eternal life is this : to know you, the only true God, and Jesus Christ whom you have sent' (Jn 17 : 3).

There is no need to say much, to think much. The sooner you manage to arrive at a state of quiet, of attention, of loving passivity, the better it is.

The advice of the Russian pilgrim is valuable in this connection. Gather up the whole of your being into a single expression of love : 'Lord Jesus Christ, have mercy on me'; and repeat it, repeat it in peace, without worrying about anything else. As a fourteenth-century English mystic put it, fashion that invocation into a sword for yourself, and with all the strength of your love, pierce the cloud of unknowing that stands in your way.

The Eucharist is like the cloud which accompanied the people of God on their desert journey; like the pillar of fire which pointed out the way through the depths of the night.

And the night shall be clear as the day.

Chapter Twelve

THE PRAYER OF THOSE WHO HAVE NO TIME TO PRAY

Every time I happen to write something on the subject of prayer, my desk is inundated with letters such as this:

'Brother Carlo, you know what you are talking about, but what you have written applies to you and to other religious like you. What am I expected to do? I am completely caught up in my work, and I have not a moment to draw breath . . .

'If only you knew what my days are like! I have family obligations, the office makes its demands, and what with parish work, parish meetings, reading in order to keep myself up to date . . . I can tell you, prayer becomes something which . . . and so on.' Or again: 'I have read everything you have written on prayer, and since it is a subject that interests me, I have given it a great deal of thought. I would like to pray, but how do I set about it? My life is one long struggle to beat the clock.

'It's an achievement if I manage to get to mass on Sundays and make the sign of the cross night and morning – but even that is done in a hurry. All the same I am unhappy about it, and I would like to remedy the situation, since I feel things cannot go on like this: I am on edge, no longer at peace with myself, and my faith is growing weaker. Sometimes I am afraid . . . '

And elsewhere: 'You have said some fine things about prayer . . . but come over to Montecitorio and you will see what happens to your good intentions about praying!'

Yet another example : 'Dear Carlo, since I became a priest, I have lost the habit of prayer – or at least of praying spontaneously as I once used to. I excuse myself by saying that it is the structure that stifles us, and it is true, it does, but I still do not feel fully justified. I am not happy or at peace with myself; I seem to have forgotten that I am a child of God, and have become a servant of the Church : catechism classes, baptisms at all hours, sung masses, and those confounded requiems that even manage to put me off the mass that I used to love so much, visits, meetings and gatherings of all sorts.

'When can I pray? The Divine Office has become unbearable for me; administering the sacraments is like working a slot machine. If I go on like this, goodness knows where I will end up. I must admit that I was much happier when I was a minor official in a small-town industrial concern, and that I used to feel more at home with my prayer when I put my advertising to one side and said the rosary with friends, or went to serve mass in the parish church without pocketing two thousand lire as I do today. That money makes me feel ashamed!'

And another : 'Dear sir, I am a young mother, and I never get out of the house. How can I manage to pray always, as you say in your book? Please teach me.'

And so I could go on to the end of the book . . .

Indeed, I think the problem is enormous if concern about it among Christians today is as widespread as this would suggest, and I must confess that the temptation to write this book came more as a result of those letters than from any idea of producing a treatise on prayer.

It may not come off, and perhaps by the end I will not even have succeeded in touching the surface of the problem, but one thing I must say : *In Search of the Beyond* is a good title for the writers of the letters quoted above, and for all who are immersed 'in things'. In order to get beyond created realities it is necessary to start from the inside. And he who is surrounded by them is right to be 'inside' – to be involved.

The mother must be in her home; the politician must be in political life; the priest in his ministry. Prayer is not an escape but an illumination from within; it is not flight but a *fiat* of acceptance; it is not a spiritual or psychological antithesis but a human–divine totality; not a distraction but a purification.

Yes, each one of us must be involved in his particular task, his love, his work, up to his neck, to the extreme limit of his powers. But God has not condemned us to work, to the family, to our social life, to destroy us but to realize our potential. God does not call us to relationships and contact with our fellow men in order to break off our relationships and contact with himself.

It is clearly a question of understanding. More often than not our uneasiness is due to confusion and want of courage. Sometimes we misunderstand what it means 'to pray'. If, for example, an industrialist, who already has more than he needs and more work than he can manage, continues to spread the net of his involvements without really knowing why, one might very well suggest to him : cut down on your work and take more interest in your soul and your family.

To the priest who is threatened with the prospect of losing his taste for prayer because of his routine and all those masses for the dead one can say : renew the parish liturgy, achieve a greater measure of participation, separate it from the humiliating rota of mass stipends, organize your pastoral duties more efficiently, and seek help from the laity – perhaps you will end up finding a bit of time to spend in adoration and to pray a bit longer.

But it is not always a question of badly organized time. One often meets people, especially nowadays, whose vocation it is to be crucified by a timetable.

In our evolving society, enormous pressures are exerted on

certain nerve centres of society, and underneath there is an individual bearing the brunt of it all : a poor woman who, besides being a wife and mother, is forced to go out to work in order to pay the rent; a nursing sister who has to do the work of three people because there is always someone on leave; or else a badly paid clerk who has to take on extra work in order to pay for his son's education; or a politician who has become the symbol of sanity in all situations and chairman of all the committees; the unfortunate teacher who leaves school exhausted, and is then eagerly awaited by all the christian organizations of the area; and finally, a poor priest who is devoured by all and sundry in a city that has lost its sense of humanity and reason.

One often wonders how people manage to put up with pressures like these. Some doors and some telephones are real instruments of torture; calculating machines and assembly lines can be real crosses for contemporary man. How is one to pray in situations like these?

I would like to write something especially for the benefit of these brothers of mine, because they have, I must confess, been something of a reproach to me in my religious life. When I found myself in the desert, having left behind me my life as a layman with its professional and apostolic commitments, one of my own crosses was the thought that, without intending to, I had, as it were, abandoned the trenches.

When all is said and done, Carlo, you have chosen the easier path. The desert is a luxury compared with some of the demands made today in the dough of the world. Yes, it is true – even granted that I have not exactly escaped to an island paradise. I used to pacify myself with the thought that it was the Lord not I who had made the choice, since vocation is his affair and he is the one who distributes the burdens.

But no more of that. Instead let us try to say something to those who come in from work exhausted, and struggle continuously in order to establish some kind of equilibrium be-

tween their life and their prayer. I would say : begin here.
Write this prayer on the back of some picture that you value
and repeat it frequently until you know it by heart. It was
written by Père de Foucauld, and reads like a simple para-
phrase of the Our Father. It goes like this :

> 'My Father
> I abandon myself to you.
> Do with me as you will.
> Whatever you may do with me
> I thank you.
> I am prepared for anything,
> I accept everything
> Provided your will is fulfilled in me
> And in all creatures.
> I ask for nothing more
> my God.
> I place my soul in your hands.
> I give it to you, my God,
> with all the love of my heart
> because I love you.
> And for me it is a necessity of love,
> this gift of myself,
> this placing of myself in your hands
> without reserve
> in boundless confidence,
> because you are
> my Father.'

And remember that Père de Foucauld wrote these wonderful
words at a time when he was wearing out the camels and the
nomads of the caravan in order to get to the other side of the
great Erg – and undertaking such arduous exploits that they
will remain in the memories of courageous and proven men.

And remember too that he repeated the prayer on the evening after he had recorded in his journal : 'Today I had to

receive more than 400 people in my hermitage. What will become of your religious enclosure, Brother Charles of Jesus?'

To receive 400 people as demanding as the Arabs, or even worse, the Tuareg – where, one asks oneself did this hermit find the time? And where did he find the time to write his famous Tamasek dictionary, and at the same time to translate the Bible into Tuareg, and maintain relations with everyone as he did? He was alone, remember, and had to build his own *sriba*, do his own cooking, and wash his tunic from time to time. And yet it is the same Père de Foucauld who writes in another place in the Journal : 'Today is a holiday and the people of Beni-Abbès are enjoying themselves. They certainly won't come to seek me out in the hermitage. What joy to be able to remain alone and to pray for eight hours at a stretch ! What happiness, Jesus, to contemplate you in the host; to put my requests before you; to love you.'

I think that, in the difficult struggle to create a balance between work and prayer, the first secret we need to discover in ourselves is this : the desire to pray. I am convinced that the desire takes the place of prayer, provided it becomes prayer as soon as possible.

It is not enough to complain, saying : 'Where am I to find the time to pray,' In fact one needs to ask oneself in all honesty whether this question has not become an excuse to cover up one's bad conscience. If I have no time, I am not obliged to go to church or to make an hour's adoration, but if I find that I can in fact salvage a few moments, then I must not hesitate. If I do, I prove that my desire was not genuine, and that my complaints were unjustified.

To pray is to love, and loving God is like loving men – that much is obvious. Words count for nothing here. If a man loves his wife, there is no need for him to explain his absences, his commitments, the fact that he has to be away. She understands perfectly well, and even though she might long to be with him more, she knows inside herself that distance cannot separate her from the man she loves.

Read the *Song of Songs* again. You cannot find any difference between the passionate love of the bride for her husband and that of the soul for God. One might almost say they were the same thing : certainly the way in which they are expressed is the same.

And exactly the same thing happens to those of us who love God. So when you are very busy, do not ask yourself whether you have time to pray; ask yourself if you have time to love.

Can love not go on living when two who love are far apart? Cannot love arouse feelings of tenderness in you every time you think about him, or fill you with an indescribable longing at the mere recollection of his existence?

Maybe I could turn my prayer into short expressions of affection, telling him, 'Jesus, I love you', while I am putting the baby to sleep; or, 'Good morning, Jesus,' when the telephone rings, 'no one will usurp your place in my heart.' Or else, in the evening, as I walk home through the anonymous crowd after work, 'Jesus, have mercy on us, we are sinners'.

No, nothing can separate me from my God. Certainly not my activities; certainly not mankind. Not even death !

And if I love him, I will find my own way of telling him so in a foreign country, and I will find a way, even if men have destroyed all the churches and profaned all the tabernacles in my own country.

Because prayer is like love : it transcends space and can be lived anywhere, since wherever you love, Love is there, for God is Love.

Think back over the story of Joseph, sold into slavery by his brothers. It is the story of a young man cut off from his tribe, from his familiar way of life and, I would add, from his way of praying with Jacob, his father. He is a slave in Egypt, sold to Potiphar, a rich man of the country. Thanks to his endurance and intelligence, he became his master's steward.

But he has not forgotten the God of Abraham, the God of Isaac, who remains in the centre of his heart, as it were, in the tent in which he himself had lived since his childhood. And when the moment of testing comes and Potiphar's wife tempts him with her beauty, Joseph consults his God in the depths of his heart, as he used to once in the tent of Jacob. You may not do this, says his God; I may not do this, he says himself, echoing that voice and that will.

If you do not give yourself to me, says the woman, I will tell my husband you have seduced me. And in order to have some valid piece of evidence, she snatches his cloak from him.

You may not do this, says the voice of his God, have confidence in me. Be faithful to the law of your God. I am the God of Abraham and Isaac . . . And Joseph goes to prison as a result of his resistence thanks to the woman's vindictiveness.

Perhaps there was something missing from Joseph's prayer?

And who knows how long it was since he had taken part in the sacrificial rites of his now far-distant tribe. And yet . . . at the appropriate moment his own prayer, his true prayer, the prayer that was like a chain of love binding him to his God, vibrated in his heart. And what a prayer it was! It welled up like a melody, like a freshwater spring, like a symphony which all the angels would come down to hear.

No, churches, formulae and methods are not essential to prayer: what is essential is that I should love, because love is the highest form of prayer – it is the fulness of prayer.

And what is more, love quickens the confidence which becomes a constant element in the soul, a mode of being, a habit, a continuing reality. I believe in him – I trust him – I love him.

Is there any prayer more vital than that? Make it your own, and you will pray all day long, even in the midst of the crowd.

Does the lover forget his beloved because of his occupations?

Are the unexpected longings that come upon him suddenly like a flash of lightning, less charged with love than the long hours they have spent together?

It seems to me that this is the secret of prayer, if one has no time to pray – and let us remind ourselves that Christ came, not to restrict but to set us free.

The more we free ourselves from the structures, from the formulae, from our idols, the better we succeed in simplifying our spiritual life and the more our union with God becomes a reality. And union is always the response to the call of love.

So churches and formulae are not an essential part of prayer, but they can help, and in the normal course of events should help. Each of us knows this by experience, and we will not be mistaken if we say that so many of the episodes in our spiritual history are connected with this church or that shrine.

This explains why it is so important that places of prayer should be carefully chosen, as welcoming as possible, clean and peaceful; above all there must be silence, and a complete ban on those strident, discordant noises that invade our psyche when it is already exhausted and severely tried by the tribulations of daily life.

And here I would like to pass on a piece of advice to my many friends who are united by their common desire to safeguard their prayer in these troubled times.

Why not make an oratory for yourself at home?

Yes, at home, where you live and love and suffer.

My life as a Little Brother has taught me to do this, and I cannot tell you how useful I have found it.

When a Little Brother moves into a new district, a different shipyard, an unfamiliar shanty town, one of those places where poor people live, and where he wants to live as a poor man, he creates his own base by renting a cottage, a hut or an attic.

After that, the first thing he thinks of in his new home is the oratory. In a corner, if there is only one room; in some other place if there are several rooms : what concerns him is that he should provide himself with a place to pray. No Little Brother should rest until he has succeeded in carving out from his abode – however poor – the surroundings that will enable him to pray more easily. These are more important than the kitchen or the bedroom, because it is there that he will find his moments of consolation, however bitter, and of prayer; there he will be able to localize, as far as is possible, his overwhelming encounter with God.

Often a mat is sufficient – placed before a wall on which he hangs a picture of Our Lady and a crucifix, and screened off on one side with a sackcloth hanging. Frequently, however, the furnishings may be more ambitious, and the result will be a delightful little chapel, receiving its light from above – as it would in a poor but peaceful attic. I feel this advice is both important and useful, especially now that cities have become so sprawling and churches are frequently far away; now that we have to exert ourselves to the utmost to remain faithful to Christ.

In this way a very busy person can more easily answer the call to prayer, find somewhere to spend a silent moment or two during the evening and a quiet corner where he can read the Gospel with his wife or pray with his children before they go to bed.

And what about considering one of those little chapels where people gather in groups to recite Vespers or Compline, or else those 'house churches' where the priest can come from time to time to celebrate mass and, God willing, leave behind him the living presence of Christ in the Eucharist?

As the laity becomes increasingly self-aware and spiritually vigorous, as the fruits of the Council ripen on the tree of the Church, these things will be realized; of that I am certain.

How beautiful it will be, the city of tomorrow, studded with those lights in the darkness – lights that proclaim the presence of Jesus in the houses of men.

PART III

'I want to proclaim the Good News by my life.'
                        Père de Foucauld

Chapter Thirteen

MAN TOO IS AN ABSOLUTE

The first time I stayed for any length of time in the desert, and acquired a taste for it, I experienced the profound longing to stay there forever, which is not surprising!

A superficial acquaintance with the world one is leaving behind is enough to convince one that not much will be lost by abandoning the city and (somewhat more difficult) its inhabitants.

The deep peace I enjoyed during the long, healing silences, the delight of the clean, luminous horizons of the Sahara, the pleasure of the solitude and, better still, the face-to-face encounter with God, were gifts that outmatched anything my youthful dreams had given me, or the heavy demands made on me by my involvement as a human being in the earthly city.

And yet, underlying this human longing to hide among the dunes, and live in a small desert *tsar* among poor and simple people, was a certain uneasiness of conscience. Do you want to remain in the desert because you like it, or in order to seek God?

Do you love the desert because you no longer love men? Are you trying to stay here because the idea of going back there is distasteful to you? 'If so, go back,' said my conscience; 'If so, go back,' said my superior. I remember one conversation I had with the man who at that time, in the name of God and of the Church, was acting as my spiritual director. 'Carlo, during these years of solitiude you have discovered God as the Absolute and you have fallen in love with him. But now you must discover another absolute: man. Before, perhaps, when you spoke of working for the apostolate, you were doing so under the impulse of nature. Now you must do it under the impulse of grace. Originally, perhaps, you enjoyed it, now you must do it because it costs you something. And remember one important truth, which made of Père de Foucauld one of the prophets of our time: one must live out the life of contemplation among one's fellow men. And if you want one phrase that sums up his thought on the subject, remember this: 'Present to God and present to men.' And so I found myself back in the world, in the midst of all the confusion, surrounded by my fellow men.

Things had changed, however, and above all my vision of man had changed. Man too is an absolute, I would repeat to myself each time someone came to visit me in the fraternity, distracting me from my prayer.

But does prayer simply mean remaining on one's knees?

That could be so convenient in times of stress.

And then I realized in a new way that even prayer can become an escape. Yes, an escape from reality when that reality is charity, love. I was forcibly reminded of this by the words of the prophet Isaiah:

'Hanging your head like a reed, lying down on sackcloth and ashes? Is that what you call fasting, a day acceptable to Yahweh? Is not this the sort of fast that pleases me – it is the Lord Yahweh who speaks – to break unjust fetters and undo the thongs of the yoke, to share your bread with the hungry, and shelter the homeless poor, to clothe the man you see to be naked and not to turn from your own kin? Then will your light shine like the dawn and your wound will be quickly healed over . . . Cry, and Yahweh will answer; call, and he will say, "I am here" ' (Is 58 : 5–9).

Man too is an absolute, and you must seek, love and serve him just as you seek love and serve God. Jesus left us in no doubt about this inexorable and simultaneous movement into the two dimensions, the horizontal and the vertical.

The closer you come to him as you ascend the slopes of contemplation, the greater grows your craving to love men on the level of action. The perfection of man on earth consists in the integration, vital and authentic, of his love for God and his love for men.

It is quite useless to look for convenient escape routes : there are none, because Jesus himself welded together into one single commandment the two elements that men, in their apathy, only too frequently separate : 'You must love the Lord your God with all your heart, and your neighbour as yourself.'

And since, with our skill in casuistry, we found it easy to separate what he had joined, he established another with the authority of his blood, shed to the last drop : 'I give you a new commandment : love one another just as I have loved you.'

After that, anyone who wants to go on arguing can do so, but he should not then delude himself that he is a close friend of Christ. To separate our love of God from our love of our fellow men is a fundamental betrayal of the Gospel ideal.

To take to one's prayers when the village is burning and the inhabitants crying for help is to create an untenable excuse for one's own laziness and one's own fear.

That is why a Church that concentrates on its own ritual and is not aware of the sufferings and anxieties of men, of the chains that bind them, is a dead Church, with nothing more to say about the heart and mind of its founder.

That is why the scandal of piety based on processions, masses for the dead, and private devotional practices unrelated to the evangelization of the poor, gets swept to one side by the protest of those who still believe in the inexorable power of the word of God.

But that is not enough. Having said that man is an absolute, we can go much further. And above all far from the bourgeois outlook which has been inherited by our generation, sick with its egoism and its racism, its liberalism, its communism and its culturalism. Each one of these 'isms' involves a fundamental denial of the absolute in man, which explains why the Christian, while he can learn something from all of them, can find in the Gospel alone a radical answer to the question of why man is an absolute.

Man is not an absolute for the racist or the colonialist, since they believe that some men are superior to others, that the whites are nearer to God than the blacks; and with the arrogance of their strength, they end up by crushing the weak.

Man is not an absolute for the liberal, because every time a conflict of interests emerges between production and freedom, production and unemployment, production and the human life of the worker, liberalism always opts for production, and condemns the human being to the slavery of irrational objects, or abandons him to the living death of unemployment.

Man is not an absolute for the communist – events in Hungary and Czechoslovakia have revealed this clearly enough – because communism, although it began with the clearly defined and sincere intention of freeing man from his slavery to capitalism and from need, is compelled to crush this wretched man every time he sets himself up against the party line, or the national interest, which is the same thing.

And, finally, man is not an absolute for culturalism, because only too often culture is self-absorbed, forgetful of the illiteracy of the masses. Someone who is bent on reaching the moon is not going to be very interested in the fact that millions of human beings are dying of hunger. Jesus alone has given convincing proof of his fundamental belief in man as an absolute; it was because of that belief that he did not hesitate to die on the cross to save him.

One final point.

The discovery that man is an absolute inevitably leaves you

with the consuming desire to graft him on to the original trunk of every absolute : God himself.

As long as man remains separated from God, he is in danger of becoming corrupt, confused, distressed, morally disintegrated.

Cut off from the source of its being, which is God, the life of man is unable to find fulfilment, beauty, peace.

Man without God is, *ipso facto*, a lung without air, an eye without light, a heart without love.

The man who does possess God fully appreciates this, and wonders how anyone could possibly live without him.

This is the driving force behind every apostolate.

It is not a question of handing on a formula, but of 'being', 'peace', 'light'.

We evangelize with our lives before we do so with our words.

Anyone who reduces the Gospel to a formula will be an efficient administrator, but a prophet, never.

Jesus came to bring fire not the catechism to the earth.

Anyone who is content to catechize, without announcing the Good News in his own life, will find he is writing in the sand, which the wind of passion will carry away. The mounds upon mounds of catechisms that have been turned inside out in our parishes and chewed over in seminaries have helped to produce the present crisis in which everything is known about Christ and about the Church, but no one any longer believes either in the Church or in Christ. The catechism, without life and without witness, is like medicine given to a dead man.

Only God, who is life and gives this life of his to those who, in Christ, believe in him, can say : 'I tell you myself, you shall live.' (Hosea). We live, by faith, not by religious knowledge, be that knowledge as deep as the ocean.

If, in recent years, our parishes and seminaries had appreciated this, we would not be confronted now with the crisis of faith of so many priests and lay people, who were also veritable mines of religious knowledge.

And it is not as if we had not been told by our fathers. The *contemplata aliis tradere* made this absolutely clear. You must pass on the fruits of your contemplation, not your wisdom, or worse still, your culture.

Only the man who contemplates the face of God, and is carried beyond himself in so doing, can effectively say to his brother : come and see, and understand for yourself how sublime he is !

To lead others to contemplation : this is the soul of every apostolate. Come and see, come and try for yourself, come and experience, come with me on to the holy mountain.

What persuades your brother to follow you is the grace of God, which is never lacking, and your own conviction, your experience, your example – of which there can never be too much.

As I prepare to speak about community, about our task in the contemporary world and our apostolate to our fellow men, I would like to sum it all up in a famous phrase of Raissa Maritain : 'contemplation in the market place'.

And I also want to emphasize that there exists no human preparation for the task of evangelization, or if there does, it is within the framework of God's plan, which nearly always eludes us.

But what does exist, as something we are all capable of grasping, is the fact that for each one of us evangelization is but the reflection of the light of the beatitudes, which shines in our faces with increasing intensity as we draw near to Jesus, the divine model. To every man who is living in darkness, evangelization comes like the moon, rising above the darkness of his way. But moonlight is always the reflection of the original source of light – the sun.

Christ is the sun of the earth, and in every man's night someone or something is needed to reflect its light, someone

who had first absorbed it himself. Ensuring that the light of
Jesus is a living reality within you is the one indispensable
condition on which your ability to shed light on someone else
who is close to you depends.

If you want to be an apostle, do not look around for something else. Your wisdom does not matter; only your capacity
to absorb the light of God that comes to you in Christ matters.

And it comes, first and foremost, in so far as you live the
beatitudes which are the most authentic and radiant sum-
mary of the Good News and of the thought of Jesus. So begin
here, first by reading them over and then by striving to live
them within yourself :

'How happy are the poor in spirit ;
theirs is the kingdom of heaven.
Happy the gentle :
they shall have the earth for their heritage.
Happy those who mourn :
they shall be comforted.
Happy those who hunger and thirst for what is right :
they shall be satisfied.
Happy the merciful :
they shall have mercy shown them.
happy the pure in heart :
they shall see God.
Happy the peacemakers :
they shall be called sons of God.
Happy those who are persecuted in the cause of right :
theirs is the kingdom of heaven'

(Mt 5 :3–10).

Chapter Fourteen

BLESSED ARE THE POOR IN SPIRIT

When Pope Innocent III, who was a pessimist by nature and obsessed by the vision of sin, wrote in his little book *De contemptu mundi* that man is like an uprooted tree, saw before him Francis, the poor man from Assisi, with joy and humility and freedom in his eyes, and he felt as though that tree had been replaced in its upright position, that man had recovered all the lost splendour of his primeval integrity. If one is to rediscover the original beauty of nature as God created it, all one has to do is to make oneself poor, to become poor, to be poor. Which means that the wealth which clings to our bodies, our minds and our hearts, makes us truly ugly and absurd.

But meanwhile let us see what significance the words 'the poor' have for Jesus, as well as their opposite, 'the rich'.

In this connection we need to begin by drawing attention to something very important. Few words have undergone greater changes of meaning in the course of centuries than 'the poor'. The Council came like an invitation to conversion from God to each one of us, and we stood on its threshold with momentous but no longer meaningful words. And yet, which makes it all the more serious, these are very words of Jesus himself.

For most Christians who talk about renewal in the Church, the word 'poor' means the beggar, the shabbily dressed, the underpaid, the man who is starving in Latin America, the children who are dying of hunger in Africa or India. That is to say, the poor are synonymous with the destitute.

This explains the watchword of those short-sighted revolutionaries, which turns the Church of the poor into an ill-defined but tough form of social action for the emancipation of the least privileged classes. But if they were right, we would be a good century behind the Marxists, who have far more vigorously and effectively dealt with the problem and not with the heirs to the one genuine revolution of love which is that of Bethlehem.

Those words with which Jesus challenged his followers and which embody his entire programme 'blessed are the poor' — I wonder what impression they must make on the man of common sense who has the other concept of 'poor'. It is like saying : Blessed are the Biafrans who are dying of hunger, blessed are the peasants who have not enough to feed their children, blessed are the children of north-east Brazil who die, as often as not, before they have learned to use their reason, or even their limbs. If they are blessed, why work to take away their blessedness? Especially we Christians. If the word 'blessed', as used by Jesus, means anything, and if it applies equally to what we understand as blessedness, then it must be contrary to his desire to work and take measures to alter their condition of blessedness, diminishing it by bringing them bread, clothes and improved social conditions.

The fact is that ignorance of the things of God has reached such alarming proportions that people are no longer familiar with even the most rudimentary terminology, and the inner meaning of the Gospel gets distorted. And this is true not simply of lay people standing on the sidelines of the Church, but of ecclesiastics who have studied theology, and who are at times, however unintentionally, incapable of explaining anything to the people.

The poor man in the biblical sense is not the beggar, the starving or the unemployed; he is the average man, who has a house, children and work, who dresses like everyone else, does the shopping and goes to the office, who buys an overcoat when he is cold and goes to the doctor when he is ill. He is the average human being – the minister, the bishop, the peasant, the craftsman, the old man, the boy, the mother, the poet, the worker.

He is everyman !

But who can claim to be poor in the biblical sense? The man who comes to understand, under the pressure of suffering or in the light of God, what it means to be human.

The man who discovers his own limitations, who enters into the mystery of what it means to be a creature rather than a creator.

Anyone, that is, who knows he is sick, small, weak, vulnerable, ignorant, sinful, needful of everything; who stands at the mercy of history and of wickedness in high places, prisoner of hostile circumstances, who has learnt humility and discretion from the pain and anguish of his experience, who is thirsting for help and for love. The poor man, in short, is the man who has discovered his own limitations. He is blessed and he becomes blessed, if he accepts such limitations as coming to him from the hand of God in order that the Kingdom might become a reality within him. Naturally the beggars, the starvelings, and the ragamuffins are included in this category – indeed they are ! – but they are not the only ones, and nowhere is it said that they are blessed *because* they are without food. Only someone who accepts his misfortune out of love becomes 'blessed', otherwise, whatever his material poverty, he might well be spiritually rich. Thus we can say that each one of us forms part of the Church of the poor, and when the community joins in reciting the prayer of the psalmist :

> 'Listen to me, Yahweh, and answer me,
> poor and needy as I am;
> keep my soul : I am your devoted one,
> save your servant who relies on you'
>
> (Ps 86 : 1–2),

everyone, whatever the social category to which he belongs, can lend his voice to the chorus without feeling ashamed of his origins, of his work in the earthly city, of his responsibilities as master or servant.

I say this, and it is painful to have to do so, because people continue to twist the meaning of certain words. Sooner or later, beset by those who believe that Christ came to found a religion for down-and-outs and that in order to become converted one must abandon the earthly city, or at least become a worker or a trade unionist, the well-dressed woman or business man will not be able to set foot inside a church.

When Jesus spoke of or to the poor he had in mind the whole of mankind, and not a particular category of men. He had no intention, that is, of establishing some kind of inverted racism or of preaching a religion suitable only for a handful of initiates or a group of fanatics. By establishing the beatitude of poverty as the basis of his programme, he brought it fairly and squarely into the wider context of reality as a whole.

Nothing, in fact, is more real for each one of us than the fact of being poor. For simply by being born we are poor, children who have need of everything; by living we are poor, creatures thirsty for everything; in our dying we are poor, leaving everything behind us. Has man not been defined as the poor of Yahweh?

And did Jesus not make this title his own by becoming man? From the crib to the cross, from Bethlehem to Calvary, from exile to work, from the misunderstandings to the physical blows.

In saying that we are poor, Jesus is not telling us anything new. This is the reality and life has been given us that we might deepen our understanding of the fact.

But there is a new element in what Jesus said : his declaration that this is 'blessed', his explanation, that is of the fact that, had we accepted our poverty in a spirit of love, peace, trust and conviction, we would have been blessed, we would have experienced some measure of happiness, even here on earth.

I have no hesitation in saying that most of the suffering in our individual lives is due to the effort required of us to face reality, rather that to any of the genuine misfortunes that may befall us.

There are some people who go through life refusing to accept themselves. I have known women who would have been wonderful people, had it not been for the complex some minor physical defect produced in them. Some people cannot even cross the road without reflecting gloomily that they are too short, or a little overweight, or that their beauty is marred by a facial blemish or a nose that is out of proportion.

It is sad to have to say so, but that is how it is.

The beatitude of poverty could liberate us from those forms of slavery too, and then, having been freed by Christ, we would be able to see the supreme beauty of the spirit shining in all its transparency, even in the face of a man who is physically deformed. That was how Pope Innocent III regained something of his optimism when he saw Francis – saw a man untrammelled by complexes, authentic through his total acceptance of himself, a man without a mask. The mask is wealth, and we can never say so too emphatically.

When the Gospel speaks of riches it is not referring to the roof over our heads or the food from which we derive our strength. When it speaks of riches it refers to the banquets of the rich man Dives, banquets from which Lazarus is excluded. When it speaks of poverty it is referring to the man who demolishes the old barns in which he can amass no further riches, in order to build new ones as vast as his own unbridled concupiscence (Lk 12 : 16–21). When it speaks of riches, it says : 'But alas for you who are rich : you are having your consolation now' (Lk 6 :24). The 'riches' of the Gospel does not apply to 'that which is needful', but to all that is left over, all that is pure luxury, all that is hoarded, refused to others, concealed.

It applies to the way we look after ourselves and exclude our brothers from the feast. And they are equally excluded when it is a matter not of food or clothing, but of culture, of the word of God, of dignity, peace or love.

This first beatitude Jesus preached in his sermon on the mount is so all-embracing and the heedless Christians of our age have reduced it to such mean, unattractive 'charity'.

The poor man is not simply the man who is aware of limits to his own material wealth; over and above this, he is one who sets bounds to his own spiritual pride and surrounds his heart with barbed wire, as it were, to safeguard it from the vanity of useless and dangerous affections.

Because – and let us be quite clear about this – if the possession of capital riches is ugly in men who exclude their brothers from the feast, much more ugly is that spiritual wealth which encourages the idea that whites are superior to blacks and keeps them away from the table of the God-given equality of men. Those who are proud and spiritually rich cause more hurt than those who are rich in money and material goods. There is no limit to the presumption, to the complacency and sense of superiority that exudes from the expression of someone who is convinced that all truth and culture belong to him. The Gospel is less sympathetically disposed to these riches of the mind and heart, and Jesus's words 'Woe to you who are rich' sound a far more serious and warning note for the 'wise' of this world than for someone who, by defrauding his brothers, buys a larger vineyard than he actually needs.

Go to the universities, go to the centres of culture, to the clubs where men assume the title of 'master'. Go into the political circles, move among those who feel they are invested with the divine mission to command, to promulgate laws, to interpret the truth.

Go with your New Testament in your pocket. You will be sickened by all this spiritual and intellectual pride, this struggle to get ahead regardless of anyone else, this lust for possessions.

There is one category of men whose arrogance exceeds that of all others : self-confident religious people who act as proprietors of religion; who, instead of serving, make use of divine things for their own ends, and instead of taking the last places, force their way up to the first, raining down the deadly blows of their abused power as they go (Mt 23).

It is not insignificant that Jesus was killed by a clique of this kind; that he felt, almost to the point of despair, that as far as the Pharisees of the Temple were concerned his message was a dead letter from the moment he uttered it.

And let us bear in mind that each one of us has it in him to become a Pharisee, capable of crucifying Jesus anew in his own heart, as long as he forgets to be poor, poor, poor.

But what exactly does it mean, to be poor?

What was Jesus trying to say when he set before us the beatitude of poverty? What a continual crisis of conscience the answer to a question like this manages to provoke in contemporary Christians!

Caught up as they are in our so-called welfare state, they feel the need to see things clearly, to understand at least what attitude they should adopt in the face of such grave responsibility. You will not find a gathering of dedicated lay people that fails to register some echo of it. Must we really sell everything that is superfluous? Can I buy myself a new coat? Can I allow myself the luxury of a holiday abroad? Must we pool everything and live like the Christians described in the Acts of the Apostles?

But the answer is not so simple, and the more one gets bogged down in casuistry, the more one senses the empty rhetoric of words; the more one listens to fanatics who would like to turn everything upside-down, the more likely one is to go home discontented and restless. The fact is that we mistake the way; and we would like to obtain the fruit without paying attention to the tree on which it has to ripen. Poverty, divine poverty, the beautiful bride of St Francis, is a sweet, ripened fruit, not the answer to a problem. And it is a sweet fruit that grows on a tree that contains within itself all sweetness: the tree of love.

The tree of love is not the tree of social justice (often it is that as well, but not always), or the tree of philanthropy; even less is it the tree of the arrogant display of one who wants to prove to me that he is better or more generous than others.

The tree of love is the tree of love, and only someone who loves can appreciate this and live the life of evangelical poverty. Poverty without love is a form of mutilation not a blessing.

Which explains why I must begin to love before I set out to solve the problem of poverty.

Yes, that is where I must start. I must love my fellow men, love them until I really grasp that they are my fellow men, my equals. Once I have learned to love them with a love that is true, authentic and uncalculating, such love will lead me on to ever greater heights. But first it will lead me downwards. Step by step it will force me to come down from the heights of my presumption until I reach the humble level of equality. Slowly but surely it will rid me of the arrogant conviction that I am better, more intelligent, more gifted than my neighbour. It will strip the mask of social convention from my face, destroy my false family or racial values – my belief that my skin is fairer, my blood more distinguished, my culture older, my religion better founded.

That is how I will become poor, poor in spirit first of all, poor of heart.

To stand poor beside the brother I love means being his equal in terms of cultural values, intelligence and human dignity far more than in terms of money. At all events, I can offend far more cruelly through my spiritual superiority than I can through my economic superiority. Do the developing nations who are just now emerging on the scene of history feel nothing of this with regard to the richer nations? And surely the

E

Alabama negro is far more easily stung by the presumptuous
condescension of the white man than by his financial superiority? Riches in the evangelical sense, Jesus's threat, 'Alas for
you who are rich', is purely and simply that terrible word ap-
plied to the man who thinks he is better than his brother,
richer than he is, and who, in his wealth, closes his heart to
love – that genuine love which looks for equals, creates equality,
makes us equal.

If you really want to understand in what sense love is a condition for poverty of spirit, just look at two lovers. Imagine
that one is economically privileged, the other culturally so, and
then watch what happens when they fall head over heels in
love with one another. The first will disclaim his riches and try
to give them to his beloved; she will play down her education
in a spirit of humility, seeking to share it bit by bit, in patience,
understanding and hope, with the man she loves until their
respective offerings balance one another.

Love creates equals, makes equals. That is its nature. Love
lives, breathes and fulfils itself in equality; and evangelical
poverty lives, breathes and comes to fruition in equality :
evangelical poverty, which, in imitation of Jesus, who although
he was God made himself poor out of love, and equal to us,
in order to enrich us with his own riches, is the most radical
expression of that love.

Obviously evangelical poverty also involves austerity where
money, food, clothing and lodging are concerned, and in this
sense the man who is poor in the way the word is usually
understood today is to all intents and purposes 'poor' in the
gospel sense, and can become 'blessed' if he accepts his neediness with love. But the subject is not a simple one, and we must
earnestly beg God for light in order to come to an understanding of Jesus's preferences, which unfortunately are not
our own. One needs to be quite bold nowadays to tell someone he is blessed when he finds it hard to pay his rent, balance

the family accounts, and has to put off buying an overcoat or a pair of shoes until next year.

And yet it is true, and in order to prove it to us, Jesus put himself in the category of those who have to cope with just such difficulties and many others besides. He was a poor artisan in an insignificant village in the provinces; he had to work for his living; he certainly had to put up with social conditions which were, to say the least, worse than ours; he had to admit that he had nowhere to lay his head; and scarcely had he given up his work as an artisan in Nazareth to devote himself to his mission, when he was obliged to submit to the humiliation of accepting help from a number of wealthy women.

But still he said 'blessed are the poor'.

Perhaps when he said it he saw further than we do.

Above all, he saw the opposite – he saw what happened to someone who was not poor.

He saw where wealth leads – and avarice, and the accumulation of money, and attachment to things.

He saw, and he could say with conviction :

> 'Woe to you who are rich,
> woe to you who are satisfied,
> woe to you . . .'

This is a serious matter, and I can assure you that, from the little I know of Jesus, I prefer not to hear myself addressed in these terms. We have good reason to be on our guard.

Suppose Jesus really is the Son of God, and suppose that everything St Matthew records him as saying about the last judgment is true : 'Go away from me, with your curse upon you, to the eternal fire . . .' (Mt 25 : 41).

I would be anxious to say the very least.

I would not feel entirely at ease.

I who love a good night's sleep, would toss and turn in my bed . . . and finally I would get up . . .

And rather than run the risk of such a terrible end, I would sell vineyards and houses – all, in short, that was superfluous – and distribute the proceeds to the poor.

When all is said and done, I want to be at peace with myself; I prefer to be happy with few possessions than ill-at-ease with too many.

And then . . . to feel one's head throbbing with phrases of the kind Jesus spoke in cold blood : 'What gain, then, is it for a man to win the whole world and ruin his life?' (Mk 8 :36).

Briefly, if Jesus said 'blessed are the poor' and if he confirmed this with the corresponding 'Woe to you who are rich', he had his own good reasons. He cannot deceive us, as anyone who has had any really deep experience of him knows.

One only needs to see where riches can lead to understand the 'blessed are the poor'.

One only needs to know what goes on in the soul of a rich man to convince oneself that it is better to live as a poor man.

One only needs to list the effects produced by this cursed wealth in a society, a family or an individual, to recognize how right Jesus was.

Ultimately, the love of God has one purpose in view as far as we are concerned : to save us.

The thoughts of God are thoughts of peace, not of affliction.

And so, since he wills to save us, he wishes us to discover for ourselves and live in the conditions best suited to the achievement of this end. The condition of the poor man is the condition most conducive to salvation. Someone who is obliged to work hard for his living runs less risk of damnation than someone else who, surrounded from birth by pleasures and plenty, weighs his soul down with a far greater burden of concupiscence, vanity and pride.

Perhaps at this point it would be a good idea to take an overall look at the mystery of salvation, and of the way God sees man on earth, how he thinks of him. We have not far to look, because in the Gospel we have the prototype of man, the unique model; the most outstanding example : Jesus Christ.

Jesus is the man *par excellence*, the perfect man, man without limitations, the man who enjoys the Father's approval.

Since Jesus could choose – he was unique in this respect, being God – when he became man, he chose to lead the life which is described for us in the Gospels, a life which is familiar to us from beginning to end.

And what was the result of that choice? What type of man did he become? He made his own the most ordinary life-style there ever has been or is ever likely to be here under the sun : that of the worker, of the man who lives by his own labour, who finds himself moving between two extremes, the two ugly exaggerations of ostentatious affluence and destitution, the man who experiences sufferings and limitations, and out of those sufferings and limitations learns the value of bread and water and a home.

The man whose dignity depends on his own toil, and not on the mask he inherits from his parents.

The man who helps to weave the fabric of society, and shuns all deceit and malpractice.

The man who bends his back to his task, and earns his happiness with the sweat of his brow.

The man who does not go in for double-dealing, who does not try to get the better of others, who is discreet, humble and straightforward.

The man who exists, as it were, within each one of us as the model of what God wills us to be. Our unhappiness and our lack of freedom are determined by the extent to which we fail to approximate to this model.

And when we look carefully we discover that both the model, made manifest in the person of Jesus, and the pattern we discern within ourselves is none other than the famous 'poor man of Yahweh' whose epic story is recorded in the Bible, which also expresses his hope and his prayer.

For is not Elijah the poor man of Yahweh? and Moses? and Abraham?

Do not the prophets express in their own lives this same poverty of mind and heart and body?

Jeremiah, Amos, Ezechiel and Micah – are they not simple men, unassuming, patient and prayerful?

It seems to me that from Genesis to the Book of Maccabees, over the centuries, that is, leading up to the appearance of Jesus, there is no room within the context of authentic biblical religion for any type of religious person other than the so-called 'poor man', exemplified by Christ in all his splendour.

There is no room for the powerful, the braggart, the self-confident, the 'self-made man', the rich, the triumphalist, the man who rides roughshod over others and lives off the blood of the poor. Or if there is room, it is on the 'other side'; and, just as in the Gospel the rich man, Dives, provides material for some sad and distressing parables, giving substance to a condemned world into which the powers of evil erupt with their full force throughout the course of history under the providential control of God's saving will, so such a man serves as a source of purification for the just man, and to try his patience.

It is as simple as that, even if, in the vast struggle that goes on here on earth as a result of our freedom to love God or not, each one is free to decide which side he will be on.

For my own part, I prefer to look for a place among the poor who have the capacity to love.

Chapter Fifteen

BLESSED ARE THE MEEK

I would like to write this chapter on the beatitude of meekness over the recently dug grave of Martin Luther King, or that of our noble brother Gandhi.

Both came close to Jesus by seeking to understand to the full, that is, to the point of shedding their own blood, the value and efficacy of the great revolution which the Son of God came to unleash on this poor earth, sick with hatred and violence : the revolution of meekness.

I would like to dip my pen in the tears and blood of all martyrs for peace, of all victims of violence and hatred, of all those who have confronted the sword of abused power with the weakness of their own flesh, after the shining example of the man who willed to offer himself as an unresisting lamb to the teeth of the wolves : Jesus.

First, then, a very brief preamble.

When God wanted to find images through which to convey something of himself to our minds and hearts, he chose two and only two : the dove and the lamb.

The dove indicates the vitality, the gentleness and the agility of the Spirit, while the lamb represents the meekness, the unpretentiousness and humility of Christ, the divine victim.

The man who prides himself on his shrewdness chooses instead the lion or some such animal, imagining, in his folly, that he will conquer the earth more quickly by the use of force and the abuse of power.

People have been trying to conquer the earth for many thousands of years, and still no one has succeeded. The fact is that the lions, tigers or serpents emblazoned on the standards of the aggressor are confronted with other lions, other tigers, other serpents, all of whom have the same significance and inevitably clash with the first. The story of what happens next is terribly simple and terribly monotonous : in the evening, when the battle is over, the two opposing armies lie in a lake of blood surrounded by heaps of ruins and incalculable evils.

There they rest a while, the worst of the wounds get bound up, the great fear is to some extent forgotten, the lion is sewn back in place on the standard with an even more ferocious grimace; then they begin all over again, thinking that this time things will go well and in the wake of victory will come true and lasting peace, our own peace. Tell me, is not the whole affair a tragic farce, to be explained by one single word : you are mad, all mad?

But then was this not the very conclusion Jesus himself came to as he was dying on the cross?

Was it not he who, at a time when people were not accustomed either to joke or to lie, said that 'madman' was the appropriate title for man? In fact, while he was dying a victim of man, he turned in his agony to his Father, and pronounced his own judgment on man : 'Father, forgive them; they do not know what they are doing.' And that is the true definition of the madman.

But do you imagine that man, who is thus defined by Jesus as 'mad', accepts the description, believes that he is mad? On the contrary; if anything, he applies the term to those who went before him, to those who failed to assess accurately the forces involved in earlier wars, who committed this or that error; but himself, mad? Oh no! and he will actually prove to you that he is not.

Indeed, speaking of madmen, who is the arch-madman of them all? There he is : the arch-madman, Jesus Christ, who during his trial was dressed in a white garment and silenced with derisive and mocking words.

You too are mad, you who want to conquer through non-violence, to win the earth with meekness.

You are mad, you who dreamed of beating down swords into ploughshares and spears into sickles (Is 2 :4).

You are mad, you who wish to turn the defenceless other cheek to the hatred of the enemy. (Mt 5 :39).

We are not mad like you, and there are some follies that we do not commit : we do not even think of them.

So runs the argument, and echoes of this tremendous dialectic ring in our ears every time people discuss the problem of how to achieve some social advance or liberate a people; how to realize a man's personal dignity or bring the human race a step nearer to the attainment of justice. And it is when one picks up this echo, deep as the heart of man, that one comes to realize just how irreconcilable are the two spirits that produce it : the spirit of the world and the spirit of Jesus.

Each calls the other mad and is answered in the same terms.

History has shown, and will go on showing to the end, which of the two is right; which of the two, the meek or the violent, will more truly possess the earth; which of the two is happier, the man who destroys his enemy or the man who lives with him under the same roof.

The incompatibility between the world and Christ is total, and I will certainly not be the one to persuade the lion that the lamb is right. I only want, and in all humility, to offer a helping hand to those who have not yet chosen between the two camps and the two systems; those who, as Christians, have savoured the beauty of the Gospel message, and suffer when they feel compelled to side with the others, simply because they have the impression that violence is more decisive, or worse still, as is frequently argued nowadays, that it features as an inevitable element in the process of history.

'If we do not fight, if we do not make use of guerrilla warfare we will achieve precisely nothing, and in any case we are not fighting for ourselves, but for the poor we wish to liberate.'

This is the dilemma, and on the walls of so many Christian homes hang the virile photographs of prophets of a liberating hope more persuasive then the liberating hope of the Gospel.

It is not that I do not appreciate the way in which they have paid and continue to pay personally for their beliefs. They are worthy indeed to take their place beside us at the workbench to inspire us, to help us with their courage and their strength of purpose.

This I accept; but knowing Jesus as I do, I wonder whether such men might not have achieved far more in the revolution for justice had they taken up the cause of meekness and non-violence.

You say that one cannot do without arms, and I answer in the name of Jesus that this is not true, that one can do without them, and obtain greater results. This is why we can be helped by the witness of those two great prophets of non-violence : Gandhi and Martin Luther King.

They believed in the beatitude of meekness, not only for themselves, but for all; not only as a subject of meditation and chosen by individuals, but as a subject for meditation and chosen by entire peoples; not only as an instrument of individual peace, but as an instrument of universal liberation.

And yet how hard it is to believe in meekness!

In no other situation more than in this one do Jesus's words apply : 'If your faith were the size of a mustard seed you could say to this mountain, "Move from here to there", and it would move' (Mt 17 :2).

Faith the size of a grain of mustard seed is not much, but we do not have even that. In other words, we do not believe Jesus. We are, without willing it, on the other side. His words outrage and scandalize us; or at the very least they surprise us : how can the wolf be driven off unless his body is riddled with bullets?

How far removed from the streets of modern Gubbio is the spirit of St Francis!

The wolf returns only to be hunted down with bill-hooks, and people want to see the pavement stained with his blood . . . and yet for a moment hope seemed to revive.

I have seen so many young people, so many women believers in non-violence, allowing the police to carry them off bodily, without offering any resistance, like the negroes in the southern states who boycotted the public transport services in American cities and travelled on foot.

It seemed that one generation had at last understood, and no longer wished to repeat the mistakes of its fathers who had cut each other's throats and achieved nothing whatsoever in the process. There was a spate of songs in which people sang of their desire to put flowers in the cannons. And then . . . it only needed someone to come along and say that non-violence was non-productive, that it was necessary to engage not in war, but in guerrilla warfare, and there was a marked resurgence of confidence in the power of arms.

How easily a bit of sentiment can change the direction of the wind for someone whose faith is weak!

As long as non-violence gave the impression that it was strong, strong enough to sway public opinion and governments as well, people professed non-violence; as soon as they could be convinced that their tactics had been understood and the powerful had grown wise to it all and were laughing in the faces of the non-violent, back came the grim, forbidding looks. The fact is that for too many non-violence was an attitude, not a faith. Fundamentally, instead of being a blessing, meekness was a pose. A mere nothing was needed to make it disappear.

I once saw a man on hunger strike. When he realized that no one was watching him, and that the papers no longer mentioned him, he went off to a restaurant and had a good meal.

So many are non-violent for show!

So many are meek in order to be seen to be meek!

Jesus would call them 'hypocrites', and he would be right.

No, the beatitude does not concentrate on results, it concentrates on the face of the Eternal, the Unchanging, the One who said : 'I have overcome the world.'

The beatitude does not involve the winning of a victory now, it depends on having faith in him who has already overcome.

Beatitude consists in being meek.

The result does not always depend on us, and we will not always be carried along in triumph. The beatitude can also lead to death, as it did in the case of Martin Luther King and of Gandhi, but it leads to a happy death and happiness such as this does not come to an end when the weapons of the violent have succeeded in tearing our wretched bodies apart. Happiness, like God, is eternal, and when I leave this earthly life, I entrust to him the task of making my blood fruitful.

The fruits may come a hundred years later, perhaps : he knows, and I know in whom I have believed.

Anyone who is unable to separate his own virtue and commitment from this hypothetical human result will be a revolutionary for this divided world but not a revolutionary for the Kingdom of God. Had Jesus been concerned about results on that Good Friday evening, he would have stopped acting meek and perhaps called down legions of angels to destroy the earth. But then what? What would have been the point of destroying the earth? What advantage could there be in ruling over a world of the dead, a desolate land where he, as the strongest, had overcome?

How would we react to him? Are you satisfied now? Did you come to win corpses?

Would a victory like that be worthy of God?

No, Jesus did not call down legions of his angels to destroy the violent and conquer evil.

He keeps to his own programme.

He too is happy in his meekness and knows he will conquer through meekness.

Time is on his side.

The last word has not yet been said on the choice man will make at the end of his earthly life.

And the meekness of God awaits man at that moment.

It is therefore a question of faith. But, as he did in the beatitude of meekness, Jesus asks us to look beyond the contingent, beyond history, to the real beyond.

We make history without concerning ourselves about who will write that history and what they will say of the men who are caught up in it. We make history, keeping an eye all the while on the kingdom of which the beatitudes are the fundamental law, and to which Jesus bears eternal witness.

If Jesus has said to me : 'Blessed are the meek for they shall inherit the earth', then I must possess the earth with meekness. Do not tell me it is difficult; I know it is, terribly difficult, because we sin through our lack of faith in the words of Christ and the absence in us of the childlike heart that would gives us the courage to fulfil totally the demands of the Gospel.

That is the reason why we are not happy, why our nights are tormented by fear, and our actions characterized by indecison and cowardice.

Meekness achieves its first victory by not multiplying corpses, and already this is in itself a considerable victory. The joy that comes from not having harmed one's brother far surpasses the joy given by some object that has been obtained at the cost of a mountain of corpses.

To end one's earthly existence in the certain knowledge that one has never caused blood to flow constitutes one aspect of one's happiness. But it is not enough. To move among men without a knife or a gun, to enter the meeting place unarmed and without preconceived fears indicates belief in a better world, it indicates the presence of confidence in the spiritual inheritance of man as he journeys towards perfection.

Have we not repeated it so often : that we believe in man, that we are at one with him?

Have we not fought for his freedom and his progress?

If so, the moment has now come for us to give proof of this confidence of ours and not to be discouraged by difficulties as they crop up.

Christ believed in man.

Gandhi believed in man.

Martin Luther King believed in man.

Why should we not believe in him ourselves? I can almost hear the reply : 'But we do believe in him, and we want to free people from the slavery of possessions, we want the poor of Latin America to achieve their liberation from the few hundred families who now hold them in bondage, we want the whites to stop treating the negroes as outcasts . . .

And so we come back to where we began. The idea that we might solve the problems that bother us by cutting off a few hundred heads does not bring us peace. We still have the impression that you get more immediate results by getting the better of someone else. Basically, we are in a hurry and do not want to accept the patience of God.

Yet Gandhi proved that he had lost no time.

I do not believe that Martin Luther King, had he resorted to methods of violence, would have obtained results any greater than those he obtained through love.

Deep inside me, I feel that all this haste is deceptive.

And if it is not, this is not something that can be readily proved from the actual effects of peace and the attempt to build on the rock of a people's patience.

I remember a story that made the rounds among the negroes

of the southern United States, part of the literature that is born of the struggle for freedom. Listen.

'It was hot, terribly hot. The cicadas were singing on the branches of the trees along the deserted street in the early hours of the afternoon. Tom, the young negro boy, had gone to the newspaper depot after school, as he always did, to collect his great bundle of papers. He had to deliver them to the distributors before going home to eat. But he always ran, and earned himself a few dollars each week without much effort. And anyway, he liked his work.

'But that day, dash it, he kept needing to spend a penny. Perhaps it was the fault of some exercise that had been set him in school and made him a bit anxious; perhaps it was the turnips he had eaten the night before. At all events, there he was out in the street with the cicadas singing, and he with his pack on his back, desperately wanting to spend a penny. But there was not a single public convenience for negroes in the whole area. There was indeed one splendid one, but that was for whites, and Tom had walked past it many times before, sorely tempted to go in; but he was terrified of meeting some great Jim on his way out, buttoning his flies.

'This time he tried it. The street is deserted. All the great Jims are taking their siestas, lying on their hammocks in the shade. Tom dumps the papers at the foot of an enormous plane tree. Then he looks round : not a soul in sight.

'His bare feet feel the freshness of the floor of this fine, white-man's toilet.

'What pleasure to relieve oneself in these cool, white-tiled surroundings ! Then an enormous poster catches Tom's attention, making him forget his fear. He wants to work out what it says. Strange how a boy's curiosity is aroused by forbidden things !

'Then suddenly Tom jumps.

'He hears the sound of a pair of shoes close by on the pavement, the shoes of some great Jim.

'No chance now to escape; you are caught, Tom; prepare yourself for a thrashing. You dared to go into a public toilet for whites. You know the law of Alabama, you must go to a toilet for blacks, people of your own race.

'Jim is blocking your escape route, his eyes icy with rage. Poor Tom, your agility is of no use to you now. Jim is strong and used to wild-boar hunting.

'One kick sends you to the ground, and then, little Alabama negro, you slip and fall till you end up with your face in your own urine.

'That is how they punish transgressors of the law, which means "their" law.

'Get up now, little Alabama negro.

'You have two choices before you, and I will tell you what they are, because I have suffered a lot myself for the cause of negro liberation. The first choice is that you should get up from the ground, clean yourself, and then, adopting a docile, submissive attitude, step out of the trap. But once outside, bearing in mind your sturdy legs, you suddenly turn round with a stone in your hand and you hurl it at Jim. Then you run off, nursing your hatred which you will describe at home to your family and intensify tomorrow among your friends of your own race. The day will come when we will destroy Jim!

'But there is also another choice, a more difficult one, and I, Martin Luther King, draw your attention to it in the name of our revolution of love. Get up, Tom, and recognize in the smell of that filth, which is the common filth of humanity, the smell of Christ's blood, defiled with spittle on the way to Calvary.

'Jim is more ignorant than cruel. He is not aware of the evil he is doing, but he will one day.

'Forgive him, Tom, in the name of Jesus, forgive him.

'It is so much simpler to take revenge. The difficult thing is to love, and you must love.

'The society we are building for tomorrow needs the binding

cement of love. We cannot go on living with a knife in our belt for ever. Tomorrow we will have to live with Jim, and Jim will understand us then as we understand him.

'It is too easy to take revenge and destroy.

'You, Tom, must build your tomorrow with the power and the violence of love.'

This is no fable that I have just recounted; it is a page of the Gospel lived out in the flesh of an insignificant negro educated by a great prophet of peace, Martin Luther King.

He was convinced that, with a people who believed in love, it was possible to carry out all the revolutions of history. And with one advantage.

If you engage in a revolution of love you will be able to sustain it, it will be lasting. If you trust in arms you will have to be on the look-out continually for someone who might want to start a counter-revolution.

A man who loves no longer needs to protect himself against anyone, since he already contemplates the face of God.

I am aware that many people will smile at this observation, just as they smiled condescendingly when they heard Jesus talk, and listened to the beatitudes.

But truth and history will not change on that account.

Gandhi would say : 'Give me a people who believe in love, and you will see happiness on earth.' And Martin Luther King would add : 'Teach a people to control their instinct for vengeance, and to accept adversity, like young Tom, and you will have a genuine nation of free men, not a population of well-dressed gorillas armed with sub-machine guns.'

But here, too, it is a question of faith, and as St Paul says, it is faith that will conquer the world.

And in spite of everything, faith gives grounds for confidence – as in the words Isaiah used when he prophesied the universal reign of peace :

F

'The wolf lives with the lamb,
the panther lies down with the kid,
calf and lion cub feed together
with a little boy to lead them ...
The lion eats straw like the ox.
The infant plays over the cobra's hole;
into the viper's lair
the young child puts his hand'

(Is 11 :6–8).

Chapter Sixteen

BLESSED ARE THE MERCIFUL

When we reach the gates of paradise, after a suitable number of years of regular purgatory, and find ourselves thronging round the entrance, along with our friends, relatives and acquaintances, and an angel of God appears in our midst crying out: 'Into your places!' I am quite certain that, to a man, we will all make for the last place, and the crowd will not be near the entrance but in the farthest corner, especially if there is a bit of shadow.

In other words, what happens then will be exactly the opposite of what happens here on earth when one is trying to catch a bus in the city, and all the Christians, sisters included, elbow their way to the front of the queue.

The fact is that during our long, patient wait in that place of prayer and peace which goes by the ugly and unsympathetic name of purgatory, we will have had plenty of time to realize, deep within ourselves, that we are proud good-for-nothings, and if at last we manage to arrive, still limping, at the longed-for gate of salvation, we will, without any doubt, owe it to the mercy of God.

And then something will happen, so unique and so great will be our joy at being pardoned, that we will no longer have any desire to argue with anyone, least of all with those closest to us, about our supposed earthly merits; rather, we will be seized by a great longing to move among the crowd, searching for someone who we once genuinely believed, before we departed from the now far-distant earth, was a source of suffering for us.

And should we chance to meet the head clerk who over-
loaded us with work, or the mother-in-law who took pleasure
in making us suffer the agonies of death long before the moment came, they will be the first we embrace, because at that
moment they will give us the chance to say in our hearts :
'God has forgiven me great sins, but I too have something to
forgive them. And by doing so, I hope to be quits.'

All the same, it is sad that we will only understand these
matters up there, and down here we will go on using our
elbows to get ahead of other people; go on tossing angrily in
our beds because we have missed out on promotion; go on
nursing an unvoiced resentment in our heart against the impru-
dent husband who dared to say : 'Don't you realize you're a
bore?' If we were to expose our hearts to the light of day and
break into their innermost recesses, what trash would emerge !
What a squalid series of thoughts and feelings, of animosity,
hatred and bitter judgments, would come to light.

And not against the Chinese or the far-off inhabitants of
Papua, but against the brother who recites the Office with me
in choir; against my wife with whom I share my life; against
the mother who bore me; against my colleague at work, with
whom I struggle to earn my daily bread.

Which of us has nothing to do or say 'against' someone?

And that is why we are not happy.

Because happiness begins at the moment in which we overcome ourselves for mercy's sake pardoning the brother who
offended us, and thus acquiring a pledge of God's mercy towards ourselves.

Blessed are the merciful; they shall obtain mercy.

Jesus himself had difficulty in explaining what this meant,
and nowhere is it said that he has been particularly successful :
our poor hearts are so sick.

He said some terrible things to convince us, but his efforts
were as good as wasted.

I have come across religious sisters who would have been

prepared to die as martyrs to preserve their virginity, but who were not prepared to expend one ounce of goodwill to establish good working relations with a nearby convent.

I have known parents who made extreme sacrifices to provide their children with food but who could not manage to make even the smallest effort to reach agreement between themselves and stop abusing one another.

I have seen bishops spend themselves to the point of exhaustion in the service of the Church, but who could not bring themselves to go out of their 'palaces' in search of the lost sheep, their primary concern being to prop up their own undisputed authority and the dignity of the Church. It might well appear from this that the Gospel is no longer read, and that we have replaced it with a thousand and one other ways of interpreting our relationship with God and with our fellow men.

Each one of us has some object of adoration, some subject he sets up on his altar : for one it will be chastity, for another authority, for another the honour of the Church, and for others it will be work or economy or a good name, canon law or a moral treatise, an old catechism or a new one, but few, all too few, are prepared to adore the loving will of Jesus, which was spelled out for us so carefully in the Father's name.

For it was Jesus himself who said to us : ' "But I say this to you who are listening : love your enemies, do good to those who hate you, bless those who curse you, pray for those who treat you badly. To the man who slaps you on one cheek, present the other cheek too; to the man who takes your cloak from you, do not refuse your tunic. Give to everyone who asks you, and do not ask for your property back from the man who robs you. Treat others as you would like them to treat you. If you love those who love you, what thanks can you expect? Even sinners do that much. And if you lend to those from whom you hope to receive, what thanks can you expect? Even sinners lend to sinners to get back the same amount. In-

stead, love your enemies and do good, and lend without any
hope of return. You will have a great reward, and you will be
sons of the Most High, for he himself is kind to the ungrateful
and the wicked.

' "Be compassionate as your Father is compassionate. Do not
judge, and you will not be judged yourselves; do not condemn,
and you will not be condemned yourselves; grant pardon, and
you will be pardoned. Give, and there will be gifts for you :
a full measure, pressed down, shaken together, and running
over, will be poured into your lap; because the amount you
measure out is the amount you will be given back" ' (Lk 6 :
27–38).

Could any words express more clearly what Jesus wants of
us; speak to us of the way in which God wishes us to live out
our religious commitment; or explain what is God's true and
innermost purpose in establishing his Church here on earth?
I hardly think so . . . and yet?

As if that were not enough, he, normally so gentle, went on
to threaten us, telling us we were hypocrites as long as we went
on noticing the speck in our brother's eye while there was a
beam in our own, and came finally to the point of confronting
us with the dilemma of eternal salvation : 'There is nothing
for it : either you forgive or I cannot save you; either you overcome your resentment or you wait for the sentence . . .'

' "And so the kingdom of heaven may be compared to a
king who decided to settle his accounts with his servants. When
the reckoning began, they brought him a man who owed ten
thousand talents; but he had no means of paying, so his master's
gave orders that he should be sold, together with his wife and
children and all his possessions, to meet the debt. At this, the
servant threw himself down at his master's feet. 'Give me
time,' he said, 'and I will pay the whole sum.' And the servant's master felt so sorry for him that he let him go and
cancelled the debt. Now as this servant went out, he happened
to meet a fellow servant who owed him one hundred denarii;

and he seized him by the throat and began to throttle him. 'Pay what you owe me,' he said. His fellow servant fell at his feet and implored him, saying, 'Give me time and I will pay you.' But the other would not agree; on the contrary, he had him thrown into prison till he should pay the debt. His fellow servants were deeply distressed when they saw what had happened, and they went to their master and reported the whole affair to him. Then the master sent for him. 'You wicked servant,' he said. 'I cancelled all that debt of yours when you appealed to me. Were you not bound, then, to have pity on your fellow servant just as I had pity on you? And in his anger the master handed him over to the torturers till he should pay all his debts. And that is how my heavenly Father will deal with you unless you each forgive your brother from your heart" ' (Mt 18 : 23–34).

In this parable we are all included; no one is left out.

He told it for our benefit. We are the debtor who owed ten thousand talents to the king. Anyone who remains unconvinced of this can stop reading this book and (a far graver thing) the Gospel. Life will explain things to him, old age above all, if he has the patience to get there.

For no one, not even God, has power to change anything in a soul that looks on itself as 'light', 'virginity', 'strength', 'balance', 'religion'. I have already pointed out that Jesus was killed by a group of those 'respectable pharisees' because they were not waiting for salvation; they thought they were saved already.

There was nothing more to be done for them, because everything was done already, wrapped up, catalogued, signed and sealed. But the terrible thing is that each one of us carries in his heart a trace of the same disease, that sense of security and self-sufficiency, of being better and more capable than others. In short, we are Pharisees. And this is the source of all our troubles in our dealing with our fellow men, of our malicious judgments and our sins against charity.

We are not happy because we are unforgiving, and we are unforgiving because we feel superior to others.

Mercy is the fruit of the highest degree of love, because love creates equals, and a greater love makes us inferior.

First let us establish three premises :

Those who do not love feel superior to everyone else.

Those who love feel equal to everyone else.

Those who love much gladly take the lower place.

Each one of us can identify his position somewhere along this spectrum, which comprises the three degrees of the spiritual life here on earth :

Death for those who do not love.

Life for those who love.

Holiness for those who love much.

The beatitude of the merciful relates, like all the beatitudes, to the realm of holiness and we have to admit that Jesus set his sights high when he had the courage and confidence to place this lofty ideal before us. It is the beatitude that he himself lived to the full, stooping, out of love, to the lowest place, even to the extent of being rejected as a common criminal, fit only to be hung on a gibbet.

St Paul sums it up so well in his letter to the Philippians : 'His state was divine, yet he did not cling to his equality with God but emptied himself to assume the condition of a slave, and became as men are; and being as all men are, he was humbler yet, even to accepting death, death on a cross' (Ph 2 :6–7).

Rather than remaining in one or other of the three positions, which is very rare, we find ourselves straining towards the beatitude of Jesus, moving onwards towards perfection, in a continual oscillation between death and life, between life and holiness; experiencing the struggle between nature and grace, the fatigue that comes from rowing with the oars of virtue, and the unexpected joy of the wind that brings us the gifts of the Spirit.

Anyone who is living in grace will know what I mean.

But at this point a word of advice might be useful, and it follows the same line as Pascal's teaching on faith, 'act as if'.

There will be moments when you will come up against almost insurmountable difficulties in your efforts, however great they may be, to love your neighbour.

Difficulties caused by his sin, his unkindness or his superficiality. When this happens, remember that to know how to love, when we read nothing but evil, deceit and slovenliness in our brother's face, is beyond our human powers – yet we are so deeply immersed in what is human. It is then that you have to 'act as if' you loved him with the very love of Jesus dying on the cross.

It is not a question of trying to alter your feelings. You will not succeed in doing that. You have to prove yourself by your actions.

The feelings follow rather than precede rational and supernatural truths. It would be unreasonable to expect feelings of love from a heart smarting under the hurt of some pain received, or of anything worse.

But we can always perform actions which will affect our decisions and our prayer.

I will give two examples to explain what I mean.

You have been offended by a relative, or at least you think you have. A fundamental misunderstanding has developed between you. You are sure you are right, and I am not disputing that. I too believe that you are in the right, that he said what he said to you out of egotism, to gain his own ends, perhaps to hurt you. I accept all that. But precisely because you are in the right, I say that it is up to you to overcome your feelings, to take the first step, to offer him your forgiveness from the depths of your heart.

Do not aggravate the wound; do not allow your attitude to harden in silence. Do not run through the catalogue of your own virtues – it will only make you suffer more. Help yourself, as far as you can humanly speaking, by concentrating on his positive side, on the good qualities you will find there in spite of the defects, on all he has done for you in the past. But above all let your soul overflow with forgiving love; feel that you are less than him, lowlier, more needing of forgiveness. See him and the offences he has committed against you with the eye of Jesus, veiled in death on the cross.

Then, with your new-found peace of soul, you will understand what the beatitude of mercy means, and you will be, as Jesus said, 'sons of your Father in heaven, for he causes his sun to rise on bad men as well as good, and his rain to fall on honest and dishonest men alike' (Mt 5 :45).

And now another example.

You are a religious, living in one of the many convents of the world. You try to get along with everyone, to live according to the Gospel. And yet you are surrounded by people who do not live according to the Gospel, who do not believe in your vocation, who take advantage of you and steal from you.

Of course, but the moment has now come when you can prove evidence for their abuses and their acts of theft.

You could accuse them, take them to court, see to it that they are sentenced.

Of course, but the moment has now come when you can prove to the world and to yourself whether or not you believe in the Gospel. It is no use consulting your feelings. It would not be difficult to guess that they are in turmoil, doing their best to sweep your charity away, like a torrent in flood.

At that moment, 'act as if' you had all the charity on your side.

Perform some concrete actions.

Do not accuse them.

Jesus asks this of you, and to put his Gospel into practice is perfect love.

Later, when it is humanly possible, you can put your feelings in order.

But meanwhile you have laid solid and true foundations for your forgiveness : concrete actions.

They make you 'sons of the Most High, for he himself is kind to the ungrateful and the wicked' (Lk 6 :35).

Here lies the solution to the difficult problem of human relations, here we find the strength to acquire the self-mastery that is necessary if we are to pass through the 'narrow gate of the beatitudes', and become 'sons of the Most High who is kind to the ungrateful and the wicked'.

Ultimately, we have to remember one thing, which is that, in moments of conflict, we must absolutely avoid appealing either to truth or to justice alone. If we do, we shall very soon find our way blocked by that same truth or justice.

Let me explain. Faced with the brother who wrongs me, who wounds, insults and deceives me, I cannot help saying, 'I am in the right.' I cannot shut my eyes and try to find excuses. The fact is that he *is* wronging me, he *is* insulting me, he *is* stealing from me. And I think and say so objectively, for the truth is the truth. But, quite as objectively, I continue : Although I can see clearly that you are in the wrong and I am in the right, I am not going to appeal either to reason or to justice, but instead follow the difficult path of love. If I do not, I will never escape from the dilemma, because my brother will counter my arguments with his own, and so on *ad infinitum*.

And here let us remind ourselves of something else. Wars are fought in the name of justice and men cut each other's throats in defence of truth, because each one has his own truth to defend.

But Jesus's attitude is completely different, and in the end we will simply have to come to terms with it, especially since he has given us such an uncompromising example. Jesus went beyond justice through love, overrode the truth by his own self-sacrifice.

He knew 'what was in man'. There was little to hide about the inner reality. It was no secret that man is a 'scoundrel', a 'cheat', a 'good-for-nothing'.

Jesus, in the presence of the adultress, the prostitute or the thief, did not beat about the bush by saying that these men and women were without sin.

Briefly, he did not deny the truth, but he did not stop at the truth. He went beyond it . . . possibly forgetting it for a moment. He pretended not to notice, he feigned ignorance like Isaac when he felt the rascal Jacob, who had come in disguise, covered with kid's skin, his clothes smelling of his brother Esau, in order to snatch the birthright from him.

'Yes, the smell of my son,' exclaimed the father, 'is like the smell of a fertile field blessed by Yahweh. May God give you dew from heaven, and the richness of the earth, abundance of grain and wine!'

But it was not his son Esau, it was Jacob who carried off the father's blessing.

What a moving 'stratagem' of love!

If God had not found the way of love when confronted with sinful man, and if he had only invoked justice and truth, how would he have overcome the great divide in order to save us? As he died on the cross, Jesus closed the chapter of mere justice and inaugurated on earth the authentic chapter of 'mercy'.

And as the mantle of his blood falls on us, it will yield an unparalleled fragrance, making us acceptable to the Father's embrace.

And so it is up to us now to use the same 'ploy', the same methods, with those brothers whose gross behaviour would otherwise make it impossible for us to forgive.

From now on, whenever we encounter a thief, or a Magdalene or a Peter, whose cowardice or deception or evil living requires our forgiveness, we will know what to do.

Instead of casting stones, and doing what the Jews suggested Jesus should do with the adulteress, it will be for us to say : ' "Woman, where are they? Has no one condemned you?" "No one, sir," she replied. "Neither do I condemn you," said Jesus. "Go away and do not sin any more" ' (Jn 8 : 11).

If we reject this way of looking at life and of interpreting the facts, we fall back on the 'juridical', 'inward-looking', 'dead' Church, which is not in Rome, although we have become accustomed to saying so rather too glibly in order to shelve our personal responsibility, but in our own miserable hearts which, instead of listening to Jesus, go on hating, like the Pharisees of all the temples and holy places of this world.

Chapter Seventeen

BLESSED ARE THE PURE IN HEART

When Teilhard de Chardin wrote his *Hymn of the Universe* and sang, 'Blessed are you, harsh matter', he certainly did not err on the side of pessimism. And it may be that the secret of the enthusiasm which this Jesuit poet and mystic has succeeded in arousing all over the contemporary world lies in the fact that he looked on the world with serene, optimistic eyes. What is more, if, as some would have it, there is something sinful in this, Vatican II was guilty of the same lapse when it decided to express its confident attitude towards the world and to state that the Church, from then on, fully accepted involvement in the dialogue, and still more in the life, the expectations and the conflicts of the world.

Naturally not everyone agreed with this, especially not the prudent. Indeed, what opinions is a prudent man not capable of expressing? He even went so far as to say that it would take at least fifty years to redress the errors perpetrated by that good-natured optimist, known as John XXIII, who made the mistake of calling the Council.

But if this were true, and the prudent man, that faithful champion of orthodoxy, were right, I would become a Muslim immediately. I would argue that if in the Church of God, the Church of the Spirit, the Church which is defined as the 'people of God', people can make such a glaring mistake, giving unprecedented and world-wide recognition to a man like this simple peasant from Bergamo, and so prepare the ground for a spiritual harvest of proportions hitherto unknown, at least in our generation, it must mean either that the Spirit is not at work or people do not understand; therefore the Church does not exist, or if it does it is dead. But the Church is alive, more alive, indeed, than ever before; the people of God are listening and have grasped what is going on within. They have acclaimed Pope John and the Council and applauded the optimism of the fathers, and they suffer because of all the cynics, the prophets of doom and the fearful, who, today as always, reveal by their fear that they have no faith.

Because it is faith that overcomes the world, not fear.

Because it is faith that tells me the Church is not in my hands, even if I happen to be a cardinal, but in the hands of the all-powerful God, and therefore, as Pope Pius XI used to say, in good hands.

But let us forget the outbursts of criticism, and turn our attention to the optimism of the Council; and to the optimism of Teilhard, who wrote :

'Blessed be you, universal matter, immeasurable time, boundless ether, triple abyss of stars and atoms and generations : you who by dissolving our narrow standards of measurement reveal to us the dimensions of God.

'Blessed be you, impenetrable matter : you who, interposed between our minds and the world of essences, cause us to languish with the desire to pierce through the seamless veil of phenomena.

'Blessed be you, immortal matter; you who one day will undergo the process of dissolution within us and will thereby take us forcibly into the very heart of that which exists.

'Without you, without your onslaughts, without your uprootings of us we should remain all our lives inert, stagnant, puerile, ignorant both of ourselves and of God. . . .

'You I acclaim as the inexhaustible potentiality for existence and transformation . . .

'I acclaim you as the universal power which brings together

and unites, through which the multitudinous nomads are bound together and in which they all converge on the way of the spirit.

'I acclaim you as the melodious fountain of water whence spring the souls of men and as the limpid crystal whereof is fashioned the new Jerusalem.

'I acclaim you as the divine "milieu", charged with creative power, as the ocean stirred by the Spirit, as the clay moulded and infused with life by the Incarnate Word.

'Sometimes, thinking they are responding to your irresistible appeal, men will hurl themselves for love of you into the exterior abyss of selfish pleasure-seeking : they are deceived by a reflection or by an echo.

'This I now understand.

'If we are ever to reach you, matter, we must, having first established contact with the totality of all that lives and moves here below, come little by little to feel that the individual shapes of all we have laid hold on are melting away in our hands, until finally we are at grips with the *single essence* of all subsistencies and all unions.

'If we are ever to possess you, having taken you rapturously in our arms, we must then go on to sublimate you through sorrow.

'Your realm comprises those serene heights where saints think to avoid you – but where your flesh is so transparent and so agile as to be no longer distinguishable from spirit.

'Raise me up then, matter, to those heights, through struggle and separation and death; raise me up until, at long last, it becomes possible for me in perfect chastity to embrace the universe.'

In these wonderful pages of Teilhard there are two key sentences, which indicate fully and unequivocally that the optimism of this great thinker was tempered by his sense of the cross and his full consciousness of the reality of sin.

The first runs : 'If we are ever to possess you, having taken

you rapturously into our arms, we must then go on to sublimate you through sorrow.'

And the second : 'Sometimes, thinking they are responding
to your irresistible appeal, men will hurl themselves for love
of you into the exterior abyss of selfish pleasure-seeking : they
are deceived by a reflection or by an echo.'

One could not express more clearly or more immediately
the reality of the evil of sin, and it is precisely on the basis
of this consideration that Teilhard begs God to deliver him
from the hold of matter, so capable of deceiving him, and
bear him upwards into complete freedom, the freedom of grace:
'Raise me up until, at long last, it becomes possible for me
in perfect chastity to embrace the universe.'

I do not know where one could find a more beautiful way
of expressing the beatitude of purity.

Today I would translate Jesus's words, 'Blessed are the pure
in heart' as, 'Blessed is he who knows how to embrace chastely
the entire universe.'

Jesus did not come in order to add to our burdens, he came
to set us free; he did not come to deprive us of that embrace,
but to make it chaste.

To be pure is to embrace things chastely; to be impure is to
embrace them in a lustful way, defiling them, violating them
and prostituting them in the process. Is that not true?

A man embraces his own wife chastely, but not the woman
he buys by exerting his male superiority.

We embrace our work chastely, and our house acquired
honestly, our toil and our friendships, but not our thefts, our
arrogance, our blasphemies, our insincerity or our intolerance.

There is a vast difference between a husband's creative embrace, and the functional embrace of the soldier of fortune who
breaks in the doors of the vanquished and rapes the first woman
he meets.

As soon as we really understand that Jesus did not come to

deny us love and union, but to raise them to a new level for us, making them even more beautiful, more human, more joyful, more authentic, we will have taken a great step forward in our understanding of the Gospel. But often, only too often, we want to try things out in our own way, and nine times out of ten, our misfortunes stem from this desire of ours to 'try', from this practical if not theoretical denial of the law which God gave us out of love.

If only those who have refused to listen to the beatitudes of Jesus could turn back! Those who have preferred to walk the way of 'possession' of material things, and who, with each new step, have sunk deeper into the quicksands of vice and guilt! Let doctors and lawyers speak up at this point; let them tell us of the painful loom on which man weaves the fabric of his sin! There is no limit to the suffering, the mistakes, the depravity and the wickedness.

And how bitter is the path of guilt! How many tears have been shed as a result of the illicit possession of things, of the violence of the strong man who wishes to become stronger, of the covetousness of the man who had and wants more, of the lust that is falsely labelled love, and the prostitution that poses as '*la dolce vita*'.

But can man really be so blind?

Can it really be that Jesus's word is only to be fulfilled in the midst of these bitter contradictions and that the ideal we glimpse through the beatitude of purity must spring from an ocean of mud and refuse?

This is the one point at which we might legitimately give in to pessimism, when those who smile condescendingly at the optimism of the Council fathers seem to be right.

Poor things! Surely you know the world better than to try and re-establish its contact with the Church?

Has your experience of history not taught you to abandon all hope and rule out the possibility of any sort of union with this 'curse', this 'world of sin' as St Paul would have it?

Are you actually planning to try again?

The thing is that in this optimistic determination to try again there is a radically new element. When they defined the Church as the 'people of God', the fathers of the Council said in effect that they, the hierarchy, were united with the people of God and therefore with those who sin. They too are on the other side, for on this side, that of the pure, the sinless, Jesus is alone, with the one exception of Mary.

They said that good and evil men cannot be separated one from another, that the Church does not contain all the good men and the world all the evil; that we are all enmeshed in sin and guilty of a covetous approach to material things.

So the hope of saving even one person from the ruin of sin is identical with the hope, given us by Christ, of saving all men, of saving the Church, his bride.

In short, it is not the 'others' who find it difficult to possess the world chastely. We all do. The bishop who is in danger of becoming a miser does; and the priest who keeps three mistresses; and the president of the Christian men's organisation who may become a notorious usurer; we all do whenever we forget to pray or depart from our God even briefly.

I can no longer delude myself, thinking that I am immune, 'saved' by preferential treatment, chaste once and for all because I have received one sacrament or a series of sacraments.

I too am a poor wretch, obliged to struggle in order to free myself from the shackles of sin; to call on the grace of God in order not to lose my faith; to remain continually on the watch so as not to be damned. This is why the fathers were right to be optimistic in spite of everything. Being optimists, they hoped for my salvation, and in hoping for my salvation they hoped for that of my fellow men.

But happiness does not simply consist in ridding myself of the hell within me, it involves establishing heaven there.

Happiness is heaven!

The 'blessed are the pure in heart' stands for something positive and expresses a profound conviction; it means living here and now in the happiness of that 'chaste possession of the universe', experiencing joy, even within the limits of the moral law and the discipline that charity imposes on me.

That is why Jesus said : 'Blessed are the pure in heart : they shall see God.'

This is the positive aspect of the beatitude, the recompense for the gigantic effort of accepting the moral commitment involved, the response to my attempts to strip myself of my sensuality, my wealth and my pride.

They shall see God! Purity of heart leads me to the vision of God. By embracing things chastely, I learn to discern in the depths of those things the features of God's face.

And do you think you are asking for something of small consequence? If the world knew how great is the joy of seeing God, it would burn the worthless bits and pieces of its riches in horror and make haste along the path that leads to him.

But it does not know, and who can tell it? Who is going to proclaim in this valley of dry bones the great hope that we will see God? Certainly not he who has nothing but words to offer.

We need to convince ourselves that today we carry out our apostolate simply by living, that the Good News is communicated by people's lives. Do you want to pass on the message of the beatitudes? Then be happy yourself.

Do you want to proclaim the happiness of the pure in heart? Then be pure in heart yourself.

Because you yourself see God through eyes that have become accustomed to the struggle to embrace things chastely, you will instil in your fellow men a longing for purity and hope for the great vision.

Chapter Eighteen

BLESSED ARE THE PEACEMAKERS

I do not know what your experience is, but I know how it is with me. When I think of my soul, I sometimes imagine it as a small boat on the high seas, but more often as a nomad's tent on the edge of the desert.

Sea or desert, either is the unbounded domain of my solitude. It is within the powers of all men to get there, but they will have to make an effort to do so.

But then I have to make an effort to get there myself; I need to sail far or walk hard in order to reach the centre of my being where I have learnt to experience peace.

I find the image of the tent particularly appealing, especially now that I know the tent from experience, and how to pitch it in the most favourable position for passing the night.

The evening search for somewhere to camp has proved an enormous source of joy!

During the day I have never had any difficulties about associating with other people and spending time on their camping sites; indeed, I have even sought them out.

But in the evening – yes, in the evening I have always contrived to place my tent as far away as possible in order to enjoy a little recollection, to savour the 'great silence', as we call it, which begins after the recitation of Compline.

In the desert, when the sun sets after the toil and trouble of the day, the wind drops and with it the burning heat and life seems to begin afresh. It is the hour of peace. On a stretch of level but not too sandy ground, beside the hillock which provides your shelter, gather up the dry brushwood of which there is no lack, even in the most deserted places, and make a fire.

That is the first thing you need to do so as to boil the water for the broth in which to break the bread you are going to bake under the sand by the heat from the embers of the fire.

An hour later everything is finished, and, restored by the hot broth and a few dates, you can throw whatever remains of the wood on to the fire and leave it to cast its fantastic lights into your chapel under the star-lit sky.

After that, move away a little and settle down in a sand-dune or sit on some hospitable rock, and then, without haste, with no watch and no definite programme, begin to pray.

I will never be able to find words strong enough to express what it means to stay with God like this, hour after hour, in the vastness of the night.

Do not deprive yourself of the experience even if the initial effort costs you something and you have to break through a certain element of coldness in the first encounter with the focus of your faith.

You will not be entering the lists alone.

Sometimes I have had to go for three-quarters of an hour or an hour before making contact with my inner self, before entering into my prayer in any real sense. I too have learned what it means to wrestle with the Angel, as Jacob did that night at the ford.

I have learned to appreciate how necessary purification is for our prayer, and that we should not be discouraged by our early difficulties. But I have also learned to savour what follows after the initial coldness, to recognize the first signs of the peace of God, to experience the presence of God and rejoice in his revelation.

There is no predictable limit set on the delights of prayer, just as there is no limit set on its dryness. These are the two unmistakable signs of God's action within us; you will never be able to control them yourself and you will never be able to foresee what is going to happen next. The action is always in the hands of God.

But that does not matter. He is God and I am his creature; he knows and I do not.

It is only right that he should sometimes stand in the way of my haste, or change some plan that I had concocted myself.

He, not I, must lay down terms for the dialogue.

In the darkest night he is the one who can see the path along which to lead me.

Meanwhile, the one thing that gives me strength to pray, or at least to want to pray, is the peace it brings.

Try it and you will see.

The resistance you put up to boredom, distractions and the life of nature round about you, your efforts to control your feelings, your imagination, and above all your desire to escape, will slowly but surely bring you into a state of true peace, a peace that is different, not of this world.

And then you will begin to acquire a taste for the reality which is forming in the deepest centre of your being; you will learn how better to recognize the least signs of its presence and to sense its unique value. Naturally you will sometimes have this experience after you have altered your own judgment about something, professed your love, renewed your desire to change your way of life, or promised to make this or that act of detachment. But ultimately it is God who brings you to understand that there is no peace where there is disorder, that it is not adoration when we make idols of creatures.

Not without reason has peace been defined as 'tranquillity in order'.

It is difficult to feel the peace of God unless one has first resolved seriously to be faithful to one wife, to pardon those who may have offended one, to live by one's own work, to discipline one's instincts and desires a little.

That a unity exists between life and prayer, day and night, thought and action, God and our neighbour, is beyond doubt, and God points it out to us so delicately, and yet so firmly. Once this order has been established, however, even if it remains a relative order, like the satchel of an untidy child who nevertheless loves his home : quite beyond our weaknesses and our problems, he gives us the joy of peace and of intimacy with himself.

So do not be in a hurry to leave your place of prayer.

Do not become obsessed with time.

Enjoy that peace as much as you can.

It will begin to shine like a light in your face. And that will be the light your fellow men will be needing when you return to them. The apostolate consists in passing on that light, not the hollow sound of your own words.

The peace of God is a light which shines in the faces of those whom the Gospel calls the 'sons of God'.

'Happy the peacemakers : they shall be called sons of God' (Mt 5 :9). I do not wish to sound presumptuous, but I can definitely claim to have seen that light. Let me explain.

Because of the damage done to my leg as the the result of an accident in the desert, my superiors have assigned me the less heavy work. I had entered the fraternity with the idea of becoming a mountain guide or at least of working with the miners in Belgium or Kenya, and instead I found myself cooking and carrying meals to those of my brethren who were doing a stint 'in the desert'. Such are the ironies of God's dealings with us !

This work, that of ministering to my brothers who were praying alone on the mountain, pleased me greatly, because there is always something more I can learn about the mystery that lies closest to my heart : prayer.

It involved taking provisions every three or four days to those

Little Brothers who had decided to make a forty-day retreat in imitation of the forty days spent by Jesus in the desert.

The Little Brothers are obliged to do this during their sabbatical year, three or four times, that is, during their lives, and it provides the occasion for a kind of spiritual renewal, a second or third noviceship. Normally speaking they spend these periods in the desert, or else on Monte Subasio, where a number of hermitages have been set up.

As I was saying, it was my task to prepare a basketful of provisions and carry it up. Naturally, when I go and find them, I look my brethren in the face and . . . well.

Solitude is a serious, demanding affair and no one succeeds in overcoming the difficulties all at once. But in general Little Brothers are used to it, and the teaching of Père de Foucauld has helped them to endure the struggle that is involved in being alone with God.

On the other hand, it is no trifling matter. For anyone who stays alone on the mountainside for forty days the alternatives are clear-cut : either one finds God and therefore happiness, or else one runs away, seized by fear and boredom. Most of the brethren I come across are among those who find God.

And so, I have discovered what light means in the face of a man who stands face to face with the Transcendent.

That this is so should be no cause for surprise – rather the contrary would be surprising – since God is God, and not a wall or a star. What, then, did the sight of this light shining in my brother's face do to me? I will tell you. It gave me a great longing to stay with him, not to go away, to speak of the things of God, and above all to listen, and to go on listening. To look into his eyes, and at his skin which had assumed a transparent quality, and to hear his voice.

Heaven does indeed exist, for here was heaven. It exists already within each one of us when we exist in God.

Enthralled by the light which irradiates from the man of peace,

I wanted to spread it. Meanwhile, experience taught me one thing : that it is not virtue which creates prayer, but prayer that creates virtue. It is very important to grasp this, because generally speaking we are inclined to approach the question from the wrong end. That is to say, we think the results depend on our own efforts, when in fact they depend far more on our long hours of patient and courageous prayer. Whenever a married couple comes to me nowadays in my cell, saying : We are having problems; we do not love one another as we used to; we quarrel frequently. I answer without hesitation : Pray more; improve your relationship with God and you will find that you own relationship becomes easier.

If a young man comes to tell me that he seems to be so weak-willed and feels humiliated by his moral failures, I try to persuade him not to pin his hopes on physical exercise, or yoga, or human considerations, but on grace, on the presence of God, on the Eucharist, and above all on the benefit to be drawn from spending at least some time each day in humble prayer, prayer that is patient and as free as possible from feelings and human imaginings.

In very serious cases of drug addiction, sexual immorality or alcoholism, I have come to have such faith in the efficacy of grace and the transforming power of prayer that I say with complete conviction : Have faith, and if you want to get better, go in for the sun cure . . . !

Yes, Jesus is the divine sun who broke through to heal the world with the supernatural power of the Sacrament.

If you want to be cured, spend one hour every day for an entire year in a quiet chapel, before the exposed Sacrament if possible, stay there like a poor man, repeating slowly : 'Jesus, have mercy on me, a sinner.'

Choose a good priest to be your guide. Make use of this time to study the Bible and the liturgy, but above all stay in the sun; let the presence of Jesus penetrate you through and through, wherever there is rottenness and wounds.

Normally the cures take place before the end of the predicted time.

Some people may smile at this, and for anyone who is unfamiliar with the power of Christ that would be natural, but I can assure you that the difficulty of effecting such miracles of healing has nothing to do with the power of Jesus which is always fully available; rather, it almost always stems from the failure to believe that a cure is possible, or simply from the refusal to be cured at all.

But in order to do this, you will tell me next, one needs faith, and I have so little or none at all. Well, I have a secret I would like to share with you. Only a few will accept what I say, of course, but it is is all the same of the utmost importance. The thought comes from Pascal, and I have put it to the test time and time again.

It goes like this : 'act as if'. I will explain. Are you in trouble, and yet have the feeling that you have not sufficient faith to cope with it? All right then, 'act as if' you did have faith, organize the details of your life as if you lived by faith. You will find that everything will work out in occordance with your desire for faith.

Take another example. You go to pray, and you feel so empty and arid that you ask yourself whether you believe in anything or anybody at all. You feel the urge to get up and go. But no, stay there, 'act as if' you were filled with fervour, live through your prayer with the same determination as if it were a moment of enthusiasm. Above all do not shorten it, do not cut back on the time. Rather prolong it, endeavouring to understand that faith relies on the will and the will on faith, not on taste or feeling. When you finally do get up from your prayer, you will find I have given you good advice.

One more example : you are involved in a sexual relationship which worries you because it has no solid foundations : either you have fallen for someone who is already married, or for someone who has messed up your life and made you the slave of your senses; or, worse still, you have been unfaithful to your consecration to God or have caused someone else to be so, and you feel continually uneasy about it. To mention peace in the context of situations like these which are, unfortunately, by no means few and far between, is like talking about a calm sea when the wind is blowing a force ten gale.

There is nothing to be done.

But there is. There is something you can do to recover your peace and along with your peace the fulness of God. 'Act as if' you possessed utter faith, unbounded hope and endless charity and cast yourself into the fray, not relying on yourself but on the strength that comes to you from your trust in God. 'Act as if . . .'

You will not overcome yourself in a day, but eventually you will succeed in doing so if you rely on deeds rather than words and if you have patience, untiring patience.

If only you could believe! Jesus would say to you.

If only you could stand before me, I, who am the life; beside me, who am the way.

'If anyone believe in me, even though he dies he will live' (Jn 11 :25).

Blessed are the peacemakers, for they shall be called sons of God.

That is what the gift of peace means : sonship of God, the authentic and profoundly interior awareness that one has become part of a family which has God for its Father and which already lives 'in heaven'.

I believe this is the ultimate gift that can be made to man while he lives here on earth, his surmounting of the terrible obstacle of fear and death, his definitive victory over the anguish of being, and of dying, alone.

Not for nothing does this truth find its place in the one prayer Jesus himself taught us to say :

'Our Father, who art in heaven,
hallowed be thy name;
thy kingdom come;
thy will be done on earth, as it is in heaven.'

And at the same time it unequivocally stamps out the subtle heresy regarding faith which would separate the Transcendence of God from his Immanence in this world.

Experienced in practical terms this heresy is perennial, but it is particularly prevalent amongst the present generation of Christians.

Either because they have penetrated more deeply the secrets of certain laws of nature and the cosmos, or because they have studied more attentively or with greater awareness the intimate bond that exists between all created things, they end up by denying the direct action of God on those things themselves.

What has God to do with the winds and the sea?

What has God to do with men's physical health, with the fruitfulness of the earth?

They have tended to imagine that, by correcting once and for all certain exaggerations or puerilities of their ancestors, they would thereby discover at least the exact point of insertion of the divine into the cosmos.

They have set about desacralising the universe and 'secularizing' the Church with such enthusiasm! And with great passion they have demolished walls which admittedly were tottering, but which none the less possessed some hidden structures that were still valid.

Take care not to exaggerate and so pass from one extreme to another. In the process of purging the uninstructed old women, who were the last frequenters of so many country churches, of their superstition and childish fideism, do not fall prey to the far greater danger of being unable to recite the Our Father and of ending up, involuntarily perhaps, outside the Church itself.

For how can you possibly repeat the words Jesus addressed to the Father, 'give us this day our daily bread', if you no longer believe that God has anything to do with the productivity of the fields and the rhythm of the seasons.

And as you go into hospital for a serious operation, how will you be able to repeat, painfully but sincerely, the prayer he himself placed on our lips, 'deliver us from evil', when you have become accustomed to thinking and believing that all will depend on the skill of the surgeon alone. Gradually you will stop praying, you will no longer be capable of praying, and even if you have not yet acquired the terrible courage to say that there is no *beyond*, you will certainly no longer be receptive to the message Jesus came to give us, the 'good news' he preached to us, his own poor, and which provides the living inspiration of the entire Gospel.

God is my father!

And if he is my father, he intervenes continually in the affairs of his son.

He concerns himself with the small things as well as the great, he is concerned with bread as much as with health, with my vocation as much as with my death. This is precisely what St Matthew is telling us in the sixth chapter of his Gospel.

'That is why I am telling you not to worry about your life and what you are to eat, nor about your body and how you are to clothe it. Surely life means more than food, and the body more than clothing! Look at the birds in the sky. They do not sow or reap or gather into barns; yet your heavenly Father feeds them. Are you not worth much more than they are? Can any of you, for all his worrying, add one single cubit to his span of life? And why worry about clothing? Think of the flowers growing in the fields; they never have to work or spin; yet I assure you that not even Solomon in all his regalia was robed like one of these. Now if that is how God clothes the grass in the field which is there today and thrown into the furnace to-morrow, will he not much more look after you, you men of little faith? So do not worry; do not say, "What are we to eat? What are we to drink? How are we to be clothed?" It is the pagans who set their hearts on all these things. Your heavenly Father knows you need them all. Set your hearts on his kingdom first, and on his righteousness, and all these other things will be given you as well. So do not worry about tomorrow : tomorrow will take care of itself. Each day has enough trouble of its own' (Mt 6 : 25–34).

Peace comes from the conviction that these things are true.